Crochet

101 Easy Tunisian™ Stitches

Designed by Carolyn Christmas & Dorris Brooks

General Information

Many of the products used in this pattern book can be purchased from local craft, fabric and variety stores or from the Annie's Attic Needlecraft Catalog *(see last page for free catalog information)*.

Tunisian Information

In different parts of the world and in different times, Tunisian crochet has been known by many names. You may know it as Afghan crochet, tricot crochet, shepherd's knitting, hook knitting or railroad knitting. Whatever its name, Tunisian crochet is a type of crochet in which each row is made up of two parts—placing loops on the hook, and working them off. The work is not turned, so one side of work, usually the front, is always facing you. Easy Tunisian is Tunisian crochet with large-size hooks combined with inspiring designs to make your crochet creations fun, fast and fabulous.

BASIC STITCHES

Variations of Tunisian stitches are created depending on three things: where the hook is inserted to pull up loops, what is done after a loop is pulled up, and how loops are worked off.

No. 1
Tunisian Simple Stitch (TSS)

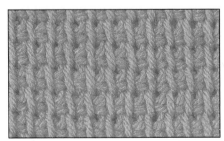

Row 1: Ch number indicated in pattern, insert hook in second ch from hook *(see illustration A),* yo, pull up lp, (insert hook in next ch, yo, pull up lp) across leaving all lps on hook. **Do not turn.**

To **complete row,** work lps off hook as follows: yo, pull through one lp on hook *(see illustration B),* (yo, pull through 2 lps on hook) across until one lp remains on hook *(see illustration C).*

Row 2: Skip first vertical bar, insert hook under next vertical bar *(see illustration D),* yo, pull up lp, (insert hook under next vertical bar, yo, pull up lp) across. **Do not turn.**

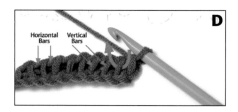

To **complete row,** work lps off as follows: yo, pull through one lp on hook (see illustration E), (yo, pull through 2 lps on hook) across until one lp remains on hook.

Repeat row 2 for pattern.

For **last row,** skip first vertical bar, (insert hook under next vertical bar, yo, pull through 2 lps on hook) across. Fasten off.

No. 2
Tunisian Knit Stitch (TKS)

Row 1: Ch number indicated in pattern, insert hook in second ch from hook, yo, pull up lp, (insert hook in next ch, yo, pull up lp) across leaving all lps on hook. **Do not turn.**

To **complete row,** work lps off hook as follows: yo, pull through one lp on hook, (yo, pull through 2 lps on hook) across until one lp remains on hook.

Row 2: Skip first vertical bar, insert hook through work from front to back between strands of next vertical bar (see illustration F), yo, pull up lp, (insert hook through work from front to back between strands of next vertical bar, yo, pull up lp) across. **Do not turn.**

To **complete row,** work lps off hook as follows: yo, pull through one lp on hook, (yo, pull through 2 lps on hook) across until one lp remains on hook.

Repeat row 2 for pattern (see illustration G).

For **last row,** skip first vertical bar, (insert hook through work from front to back between strands of next vertical bar, yo, pull through 2 lps on hook) across. Fasten off.

No. 3
Tunisian Purl Stitch (TPS)

Row 1: Ch number indicated in pattern, bring yarn to front of work (see illustration H); working behind yarn, insert hook in second ch from hook, yo, pull up lp, (insert hook in next ch, yo, pull up lp) across leaving all lps on hook. **Do not turn.**

To **complete row,** work lps off hook as follows: yo, pull through one lp on hook, (yo, pull through

2 lps on hook) across until one lp remains on hook.

Note: Photos H through K show working Tunisian Purl Stitch after two rows of Tunisian Simple Stitch have been completed.

Row 2: Skip first vertical bar, bring yarn to front of work; working behind yarn, insert hook under next vertical bar, yo, pull up lp (see illustration I) across. **Do not** turn.

To **complete row,** work lps off as follows: yo, pull through one lp on hook (see illustration J), (yo, pull through 2 lps on hook) across until one lp remains on hook (see illustration K).

Repeat row 2 for pattern.

For **last row,** skip first vertical bar, (bring yarn to front of work; working behind yarn, insert hook under next vertical bar, yo, pull through 2 lps on hook) across. Fasten off.

No. 4
Tunisian Mesh Stitch (TMS)

Row 1: Ch number indicated in pattern *(desired number of sts plus 1)*, insert hook in third ch from hook, yo, pull up lp, ch 1, (insert hook in next ch, yo, pull up lp, ch 1) across leaving all lps on hook. **Do not turn.**

To **complete row,** work lps off hook as follows: yo, pull through one lp on hook, (yo, pull through 2 lps on hook) across until one lp remains on hook.

Row 2: Ch 1, skip first vertical bar, (insert hook in horizontal bar slightly above and behind next vertical bar, yo, pull up lp, ch 1) across. **Do not turn.**

To **complete row,** work lps off as follows: yo, pull through one lp on hook, (yo, pull through 2 lps on hook) across until one lp remains on hook.

Repeat row 2 for pattern.

For **last row,** ch 1, skip first vertical bar, (insert hook in horizontal bar slightly above and behind next vertical bar, yo, pull through 2 lps on hook) across. Fasten off.

No. 5
Tunisian Double Stitch (TDS)

Row 1: Ch number indicated in pattern *(desired number of sts plus 1)*, yo, insert hook in third ch from hook, yo, pull up lp, yo, pull through 2 lps on hook *(this is like making a double crochet without drawing through last 2 lps on hook)*, (yo, insert hook in next ch, yo, pull up lp, yo, pull through 2 lps on hook) across leaving all lps on hook. **Do not turn.**

To **complete row,** work lps off as follows: yo, pull through one

lp on hook, (yo, pull through 2 lps on hook) across until one lp remains on hook.

Row 2: Ch 1, skip first vertical bar, (yo, insert hook under next vertical bar, yo, pull up lp, yo, pull through 2 lps on hook) across. **Do not turn.**

To **complete row,** work lps off as follows: yo, pull through one lp on hook, (yo, pull through 2 lps on hook) across until one lp remains on hook.

Repeat row 2 for pattern.

For **last row,** ch 1, hdc or dc in each vertical bar across as indicated in pattern. Fasten off.

No. 6
Tunisian Reverse Stitch (TRS)

Row 1: Ch number indicated in pattern *(desired number of sts plus 1)*, insert hook in third ch from hook, yo, pull up lp, ch 1, (insert hook in next ch, yo, pull up lp, ch 1) across leaving all lps on hook. **Do not turn.**

To **complete row,** work lps off hook as follows: yo, pull through one lp on hook, (yo, pull through 2 lps on hook) across until one lp remains on hook.

Row 2: Skip first vertical bar, insert hook through work from back to front between strands of next vertical bar *(see illustration)*, yo,

pull up lp, (insert hook from back to front between strands of next vertical bar, yo, pull up lp) across. **Do not turn.**

To **complete row,** work lps off as follows: yo, pull through one lp on hook, (yo, pull through 2 lps on hook) across until one lp remains on hook.

Repeat row 2 for pattern.

For **last row,** skip first vertical bar, (insert hook through work from back to front between strands of next vertical bar, yo, pull through 2 lps on hook) across. Fasten off.

No. 7
Tunisian Extended Stitch (TES)

Row 1: Ch number indicated in pattern, insert hook in second ch from hook, yo, pull up lp, ch 1, (insert hook in next ch, yo, pull up lp, ch 1) across leaving all lps on hook. **Do not turn.**

To **complete row,** work lps off hook as follows: yo, pull through one lp on hook, (yo, pull through 2 lps on hook) across until one lp remains on hook.

Row 2: Ch 1, skip first vertical bar, insert hook under next vertical bar, yo, pull up lp, ch 1, (insert hook under next vertical bar, yo, pull up lp, ch 1) across. **Do not turn.**

To **complete row,** work lps off as follows: yo, pull through one lp on hook, (yo, pull through 2 lps on hook) across until one lp remains on hook.

Repeat row 2 for pattern.

For **last row,** sl st in each vertical bar across. Fasten off.❏❏

Tips for Beautiful Easy Tunisian Stitching

Beginning and Ending
Beginning chain, last row and borders are worked with hook one size smaller than hook used for remainder of design. If these important edge stitches are worked with the larger size hook, edges are often loose and rippled. Using the smaller hook allows you to achieve straight, square Easy Tunisian edges.

Taming the Curl
Tunisian stitch pieces tend to curl, but there are several things you can do to lessen the curl. When working first row, pick up loops by inserting hook through the **back bar** of each beginning chain (see illustration L).

To further counteract the curl, before assembling afghan parts or parts of a sweater, steam lightly. Lay piece on towel or other padded surface and steam by holding iron near stitches and allowing steam to penetrate. Do not allow iron to touch stitches. Flatten and smooth with fingers if needed. Allow piece to dry in this position. Curling is

also lessened by working one or two rows of Tunisian Purl Stitch before beginning rows of Tunisian Simple Stitch. Adding a border is also effective.

Right Edge
If the stitches along right edge are too loose as you work; use this method to make a flawless, firm right edge.

A. For rows of Tunisian Simple Stitch, purl stitch, knit stitch and other similar stitches:

At beginning of row, place the single lp on a large safety pin.

Pull up lps as indicated in pattern for remainder of row (see illustration M).

Work off lps as indicated in pattern until you have one lp on hook. Remove hook from lp, place safety-pinned lp on hook. Place dropped lp on hook (see illustration N)

Remove pin. Work off these lps as indicated in pattern.

To **begin next row,** place remaining lp on safety pin. Pull up lp in second vertical bar (see illustration O). Complete row.

Work remaining rows in same manner, beginning each row by placing lp on hook onto safety pin.

B. For rows of Double Tunisian Stitch, Lace Stitch and other similar stitches, complete the action indicated in pattern before beginning next stitch (usually ch 1). Place safety pin on resulting loop.❑❑

1

Puffs,
Pebbles &
Popcorn

MATERIALS
❑ Desired color yarn
❑ Easy Tunisian hook

SPECIAL STITCH
For **bobble,** yo, insert hook from front to back between strands of next vertical bar, yo, pull lp through, yo, pull through 2 lps on hook, *yo, insert hook in same sp, yo, pull lp through, yo, pull through 2 lps on hook; repeat from * one more time, yo, pull through 3 lps on hook, ch 1.

NOTE
Read Tunisian Information on pages 1–4 before beginning pattern.

STITCH PATTERN
Row 1: Ch a minimum of 21 or in multiples of 16 plus 5, pull up lp in second ch from hook, pull up lp in each ch across, **do not turn;** work lps off hook.
Row 2: Work in TSS.
Row 3: Skip first vertical bar, TSS in next vertical bar, **bobble** (see

Special Stitch), (TSS in next 15 vertical bars, bobble) across to last 2 vertical bars, TSS in last 2 vertical bars; work lps off hook.
Row 4: Work in TSS.
Row 5: Skip first vertical bar, TSS in next vertical bar, bobble, (TSS in next 7 vertical bars, bobble) across to last 2 vertical bars, TSS in last 2 vertical bars; work lps off hook.

Row 6: Work in TSS.
Row 7: Skip first vertical bar, TSS in next vertical bar, bobble, *TSS in next 5 vertical bars, bobble, TSS in next 3 vertical bars, bobble, TSS in next 5 vertical bars, bobble; repeat from * across to last 2 vertical bars, TSS in last 2 vertical bars; work lps off hook.
Row 8: Work in TSS.
Row 9: Skip first vertical bar, TSS in next vertical bar, bobble, (TSS in next 3 vertical bars, bobble) across to last 2 vertical bars, TSS in last 2 vertical bars; work lps off hook.
Row 10: Work in TSS.
Row 11: Repeat row 7.
Row 12: Work in TSS.
Row 13: Repeat row 5.
Rows 14 & 15: Work in TSS.
Pattern Rows: Repeat rows 3–15 consecutively to desired size.
Last Row: Skip first vertical bar, insert hook in next vertical bar, yo, pull through 2 lps on hook (sl st completed), sl st in each vertical bar across. Fasten off.❑❑

MATERIALS
❑ Desired color yarn
❑ Easy Tunisian hook

SPECIAL STITCH
For **puff st,** yo, insert hook around both strands of next vertical bar, yo, pull lp through, (yo, insert hook around both strands of same vertical bar, yo, pull lp through) 2 times, yo, pull through 6 lps on hook, ch 1.

NOTE
Read Tunisian Information on pages 1–4 before beginning pattern.

STITCH PATTERN
Row 1: Ch a minimum of 15 or in multiples of 4 plus 3, pull up

lp in second ch from hook, pull up lp in each ch across, **do not turn;** work lps off hook.

Row 2: Skip first vertical bar, TSS in next 2 vertical bars, **puff st** (see Special Stitch), TSS in next 3 vertical bars, (puff st, TSS in next 3 vertical bars) across; work lps off hook.
Row 3: Work in TSS.
Row 4: Skip first vertical bar, TSS in next 4 vertical bars, puff st, (TSS in next 3 vertical bars, puff st) across to last 5 vertical bars, TSS in last 5 vertical bars; work lps off hook.
Row 5: Work in TSS.
Pattern Rows: Repeat rows 2–5 consecutively to desired length.
Last Row: Skip first vertical bar, insert hook in next vertical bar, yo, pull through 2 lps on hook (sl st completed), sl st in each vertical bar across. Fasten off.❑❑

MATERIALS
- ❑ Desired color yarn
- ❑ Easy Tunisian hook

SPECIAL STITCH
For **long double crochet-loop cluster (ldc-lp cluster),** yo, insert hook around both strands at base of designated vertical bar, yo, pull up long lp, yo, pull through 2 lps on hook, (yo, insert hook around both strands of same vertical bar, yo, pull up long lp, yo, pull through 2 lps on hook) 2 times, yo, pull through 3 lps on hook.

NOTE
Read Tunisian Information on pages 1–4 before beginning pattern.

STITCH PATTERN
Row 1: Ch a minimum of 11 or

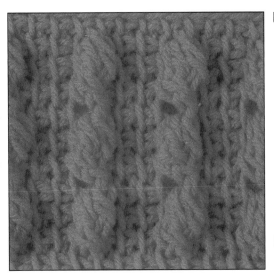

in multiples of 4 plus 3, pull up lp in second ch from hook, pull up lp in each ch across, **do not turn;** work lps off hook.

Rows 2–4: Work in TSS.

Row 5: Skip first vertical bar, TSS in next 2 vertical bars, **ldc-lp cluster** (see Special Stitch) around next vertical bar 3 rows before last, pull up lp in vertical bar on last row behind cluster, yo, pull through 2 lps on hook, TSS in next 3 vertical bars, *ldc-lp cluster around next vertical bar 3 rows before last, pull up lp in vertical bar on last row behind cluster, yo, pull through 2 lps on hook, TSS in next 3 vertical bars; repeat from * across; work lps off hook.

Pattern Rows: Repeat rows 2–5 consecutively to desired size, ending with row 2.

Last Row: Skip first vertical bar, insert hook in next vertical bar, yo, pull through 2 lps on hook (sl st completed), sl st in each vertical bar across. Fasten off.❑❑

MATERIALS
- ❑ Desired color yarn
- ❑ Easy Tunisian hook

SPECIAL STITCH
For **puff st,** yo, insert hook around both strands of next vertical bar, yo, pull lp through, (yo, insert hook around both strands of same vertical bar, yo, pull lp through) 2 times, yo, pull through 6 lps on hook, ch 1.

NOTE
Read Tunisian Information on pages 1–4 before beginning pattern.

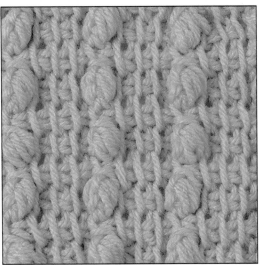

STITCH PATTERN
Row 1: Ch a minimum of 11 or in multiples of 4 plus 3, pull up lp in second ch from hook, pull up lp in each ch across, **do not turn;** work lps off hook.

Row 2: Skip first vertical bar, TSS in next 2 vertical bars, **puff st** (see Special Stitch), TSS in next 3 vertical bars, (puff st, TSS in next 3 vertical bars) across; work lps off hook.

Row 3: Work in TSS.

Pattern Rows: Repeat rows 2 and 3 alternately to desired size.

Last Row: Skip first vertical bar, insert hook in next vertical bar, yo, pull through 2 lps on hook (sl st completed), sl st in each vertical bar across. Fasten off.❑❑

MATERIALS
❑ Desired color yarn
❑ Easy Tunisian hook

SPECIAL STITCH
For **bobble,** yo, insert hook from front to back between strands of next vertical bar, yo, pull lp through, yo, pull through 2 lps on hook, *yo, insert hook in same sp, yo, pull lp through, yo, pull through 2 lps on hook; repeat from * one more time, yo, pull through 3 lps on hook, ch 1.

NOTE
Read Tunisian Information on page 1–4 before beginning pattern.

STITCH PATTERN
Row 1: Ch a minimum of 27 or in multiples of 8 plus 3, pull up lp in second ch from hook, pull up lp in each ch across, **do not turn;** work lps off hook.
Rows 2 & 3: Work in TKS.
Row 4: Skip first vertical bar, TKS in next 4 vertical bars, **bobble** *(see Special Stitch),* (TKS in next

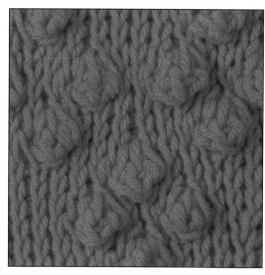

7 vertical bars, bobble) across to last 5 vertical bars, TKS in last 5 vertical bars; work lps off hook.
Row 5: Work in TKS.
Row 6: Skip first vertical bar, TKS in next 2 vertical bars, (bobble, TKS in next 3 vertical bars) across; work lps off hook.
Row 7: Work in TKS.
Row 8: Skip first vertical bar, TKS in next 4 vertical bars, bobble, (TKS in next 7 vertical bars, bobble)

across to last 5 vertical bars, TKS in last 5 vertical bars; work lps off hook.
Row 9: Work in TKS across.
Row 10: Skip first vertical bar, TKS in next 8 vertical bars, bobble, (TKS in next 7 vertical bars, bobble) across to last 9 vertical bars, TKS in last 9 vertical bars; work lps off hook.
Row 11: Work in TKS across.
Row 12: Skip first vertical bar, TKS in next 6 vertical bars, bobble, (TKS in next 3 vertical bars, bobble) across to last 7 vertical bars, TKS in last 7 vertical bars; work lps off hook.
Row 13: Work in TKS across.
Row 14: Repeat row 10.
Row 15: Work in TKS across.
Pattern Rows: Repeat rows 4–15 consecutively to desired size.
Last Row: Skip first vertical bar, *insert hook through work from front to back between strands of next vertical bar, yo, pull through 2 lps on hook *(sl st completed);* repeat from * across. Fasten off.❑❑

MATERIALS
❑ Desired color yarn
❑ Easy Tunisian hook

SPECIAL STITCH
For **extended-treble crochet (ext)**, yo 2 times, insert hook in designated vertical bar, yo, pull up lp, yo, pull through one lp on hook, (yo, pull through 2 lps on hook) 2 times.

NOTE
Read Tunisian Information on page 1–4 before beginning pattern.

STITCH PATTERN
Row 1: Ch in multiples of 2 plus 1, pull up lp in second ch from hook, pull up lp in each ch across, **do not turn;** work lps off hook.
Row 2: Work in TSS.

Row 3: Skip first vertical bar, **ext** *(see Special Stitch)* around both strands at base of next vertical bar, insert hook through one strand only at top of same vertical bar, yo, pull lp through strand and lp on hook *(sl st completed)*, TSS in next vertical bar, (ext around both strands at base of next vertical bar, sl st in one strand only at top of same vertical bar, TSS in next vertical bar) across; work lps off hook.
Row 4: Skip first vertical bar, (TSS in next vertical bar, ext around both strands at base of next vertical bar, sl st on one strand only at top of same vertical bar) across to last 2 vertical bars, TSS in last 2 vertical bars; work lps off hook.
Pattern Rows: Repeat rows 3 and 4 alternately to desired size.
Next Row: Work in TSS.
Last Row: Skip first vertical bar, insert hook in next vertical bar, yo, pull through 2 lps on hook *(sl st completed)*, sl st in each vertical bar across. Fasten off.❑❑

MATERIALS
❑ Desired color yarn
❑ Easy Tunisian hook

SPECIAL STITCH
For **popcorn (pc)**, yo, insert hook through work between front and back strands of next vertical bar, yo, pull lp through, yo, pull through 2 lps on hook, (yo, insert hook in same sp, yo, pull lp through, yo, pull through 2 lps on hook) 2 times, yo, pull through 3 lps on hook, ch 1.

NOTE
Read Tunisian Information on page 1–4 before beginning pattern.

STITCH PATTERN
Row 1: Ch a minimum of 33 or in multiples of 14 plus 5, pull up lp in second ch from hook, pull up lp in each ch across, **do not turn;** work lps off hook.
Rows 2–5: Work in TSS.

Row 6: Skip first vertical bar, TSS in next 8 vertical bars, **pc** *(see Special Stitch)*, (TSS in next 13 vertical bars, pc) across to last 9 vertical bars, TSS in last 9 vertical bars; to **work lps off hook,** yo, pull through one lp on hook, (yo, pull through 2 lps on hook) 7 times, ch 8, (yo, pull through 2 lps on hook) 3 times, ch 8, *(yo, pull through 2 lps on hook) 11 times, ch 8, (yo, pull through 2 lps on hook) 3 times, ch 8; repeat from * across to last 8 lps on hook, (yo, pull through 2 lps on hook) 8 times.
Rows 7 & 8: Skipping ch lps and pulling ch lps to front, work in TSS.
Row 9: Skip first vertical bar, TSS in next 4 vertical bars, *(insert hook through next ch lp 3 rows below and in next vertical bar at same time, yo, pull up lp), TSS in next 7 vertical bars; repeat between ( ), TSS in next 5 vertical bars; repeat from * across; work lps off hook.
Rows 10–12: Work in TSS.
Pattern Rows: Repeat rows 6–12 consecutively to desired size.
Last Row: Skip first vertical bar, insert hook in next vertical bar, yo, pull through 2 lps on hook *(sl st completed)*, sl st in each vertical bar across. Fasten off.❑❑

MATERIALS
- ❑ Desired color yarn
- ❑ Easy Tunisian hook

SPECIAL STITCH
For **popcorn (pc),** yo, insert hook through work between front and back strands of next vertical bar, yo, pull lp through, yo, pull through 2 lps on hook, (yo, insert hook in same sp, yo, pull lp through, yo, pull through 2 lps on hook) 2 times, yo, pull through 3 lps on hook, ch 1.

NOTE
Read Tunisian Information on pages 1–4 before beginning pattern.

STITCH PATTERN
Row 1: Ch a minimum of 33 or in multiples of 14 plus 5, pull up lp in second ch from hook, pull up lp in each ch across, **do not turn;** work lps off hook.

Rows 2 & 3: Work in TSS.

Row 4: Skip first vertical bar, TSS in each vertical bar across; to **work lps off hook,** yo, pull through one lp on hook, (yo, pull through 2 lps on hook) 4 times, *ch 8, (yo, pull through 2 lps on hook)

9 times, ch 8, (yo, pull through 2 lps on hook) 5 times; repeat from * across.

Rows 5 & 6: Skipping ch lps and pulling ch lps to front, work in TSS.

Row 7: Skip first vertical bar, TSS in next 6 vertical bars, [*(insert hook through next ch lp 3 rows below and in next vertical bar at same time, yo, pull up lp), TSS in next 3 vertical bars; repeat between ( )*, TSS in next 9 vertical bars]; repeat between [ ] across to last 12 vertical bars; repeat between **, TSS in last 7 vertical bars; work lps off hook.

Row 8: Skip first vertical bar, TSS in next 8 vertical bars, **pc** (see Special Stitch), (TSS in next 13 vertical bars, pc) across to last 9 vertical bars, TSS in last 9 vertical bars; to **work lps off hook,** yo, pull through one lp on hook, (yo, pull through 2 lps on hook) 7 times, *(yo, pull through 2 lps on hook) 11 times, ch 8, (yo, pull through 2 lps on hook) 3 times, ch 8; repeat from * across to last 8 lps on hook, (yo, pull through 2 lps on hook) 8 times.

Rows 9 & 10: Skipping ch lps and pulling ch lps to front, work in TSS.

Row 11: Skip first vertical bar, TSS in next 4 vertical bars, *(insert hook through next ch lp 3 rows below and in next vertical bar at same time, yo, pull up lp), TSS in next 7 vertical bars; repeat between ( ), TSS in next 5 vertical bars; repeat from * across; work lps off hook.

Pattern Rows: Repeat rows 2–11 consecutively to desired size.

Last Row: Skip first vertical bar, insert hook in next vertical bar, yo, pull through 2 lps on hook (sl st completed), sl st in each vertical bar across. Fasten off.❑❑

MATERIALS
- ❑ Desired color yarn
- ❑ Easy Tunisian hook

NOTES
Read Tunisian Information on pages 1–4 before beginning pattern.

This sample block demonstrates the pebble stitch. The ch-3 sps made when working lps off hook form the pebble stitch pattern.

You can achieve a different look by pushing the ch-3 sps to the back and using the wrong side as the front.

STITCH PATTERN—SAMPLE BLOCK
Row 1: Ch 20, pull up lp in second ch from hook, pull up lp in each ch across, **do not turn;** work lps off hook.

Rows 2–4: Work in TSS.

Row 5: Skip first vertical bar, TSS in each vertical bar across; to **work lps off hook,** yo, pull through one lp on hook, (yo, pull through 2 lps on hook) 9 times, ch 3, (yo, pull through 2 lps on hook) 10 times.

Row 6: Skip first vertical bar, TSS in each vertical bar across; to **work lps off hook,** yo, pull through one lp on hook, (yo, pull through 2 lps on hook) 8 times, ch 3, (yo, pull through 2 lps on hook) 2 times, ch 3, (yo, pull through 2 lps on hook) 9 times.

Row 7: Skip first vertical bar, TSS in each vertical bar across; to **work lps off hook,** yo, pull through one lp on hook, (yo, pull through 2 lps on hook) 7 times, ch 3, (yo, pull through 2 lps on hook) 4 times, ch 3, (yo, pull through 2 lps on hook) 8 times.

Row 8: Skip first vertical bar, TSS in each vertical bar across; to **work lps off hook,** yo, pull through one lp on hook, (yo, pull through 2 lps on hook) 6 times, ch 3, (yo, pull through 2 lps on hook) 6 times, ch 3, (yo, pull through 2 lps on hook) 7 times.

Row 9: Skip first vertical bar, TSS in each vertical bar across; to **work lps off hook,** yo, pull through one lp on hook, (yo, pull through 2 lps on hook) 5 times, ch 3, (yo, pull through 2 lps on hook) 8 times, ch 3, (yo, pull through 2 lps on hook) 6 times.

Row 10: Repeat row 8.

Row 11: Repeat row 7.

Row 12: Repeat row 6.

Row 13: Repeat row 5.

Rows 14–18: Work in TSS.

Pattern Rows: Repeat rows 5–18 consecutively to desired size.

Last Row: Skip first vertical bar, insert hook in next vertical bar, yo, pull through 2 lps on hook *(sl st completed),* sl st in each vertical bar across. Fasten off.❑❑

MATERIALS
- ❑ Desired color yarn
- ❑ Easy Tunisian hook

SPECIAL STITCH
For **bobble,** yo, insert hook from front to back between strands of next vertical bar, yo, pull lp through, yo, pull through 2 lps on hook, *yo, insert hook in same sp, yo, pull lp through, yo, pull through 2 lps on hook; repeat from * one more time, yo, pull through 3 lps on hook, ch 1.

NOTE
Read Tunisian Information on pages 1–4 before beginning pattern.

STITCH PATTERN
Row 1: Ch a minimum of 13 or in multiples of 6 plus 1, pull up lp in second ch from hook, pull up lp in each ch across, **do not turn;** work lps off hook.

Row 2: Work in TSS.

Row 3: Skip first vertical bar, TSS in next 2 vertical bars, **bobble** *(see Special Stitch),* (TSS in next 5 vertical bars, bobble) across to last 3 vertical bars, TSS in last 3 vertical bars; work lps off hook.

Pattern Rows: Repeat rows 2 and 3 alternately to desired size, ending with row 2.

Last Row: Skip first vertical bar, insert hook in next vertical bar, yo, pull through 2 lps on hook *(sl st completed),* sl st in each vertical bar across. Fasten off.❑❑

MATERIALS
❑ Desired color yarn
❑ Easy Tunisian hook

SPECIAL STITCHES
For **double crochet loop (dc lp),** yo, insert hook in specified vertical bar, yo, pull lp through, yo, pull through 2 lps on hook.

For **treble crochet lp (tr lp),** yo 2 times, insert hook from front to back around post of next dc lp, yo, pull lp through, (yo, pull through 2 lps on hook) 2 times.

For **double crochet-loop cluster (dc-lp cluster),** yo, insert hook around both strands at base of designated vertical bar, yo, pull lp through, yo, pull through 2 lps on hook, (yo, insert hook around both strands of same vertical bar, yo, pull lp through, yo, pull through 2 lps on hook) 2 times, yo, pull through 3 lps on hook, ch 1.

NOTE
Read Tunisian Information on pages 1–4 before beginning pattern.

STITCH PATTERN
Row 1: Ch a minimum of 13 or in multiples of 6 plus 1, pull up lp in second ch from hook, pull up lp in each ch across, **do not turn;** work lps off hook.
Rows 2 & 3: Work in TSS.
Row 4: Skip first vertical bar, TSS

in next 2 vertical bars, **dc lp** *(see Special Stitches)* in next vertical bar on row before last, skip next vertical bar on last row, (TSS in next 5 vertical bars, dc lp in next vertical bar on row before last, skip next vertical bar on last row) across to last 3 vertical bars, TSS in last 3 vertical bars; work lps off hook.
Rows 5 & 6: Skip first vertical bar, TSS in next 2 vertical bars, **tr lp** *(see Special Stitches)* around next dc lp or tr lp, (TSS in next 5 vertical bars, tr lp around next dc lp or tr lp) across to last 3 vertical bars, TSS in last 3 vertical bars; work lps off hook.
Row 7: Skip first vertical bar, TSS in next 2 vertical bars, **dc-lp cluster** *(see Special Stitches)* around next tr lp, *TSS in next 2 vertical bars, dc lp in vertical bar on row

before last, skip next vertical bar on last row, TSS in next 2 vertical bars, dc-lp cluster around next tr lp; repeat from * across to last 3 vertical bars, TSS in last 3 vertical bars; work lps off hook.
Rows 8 & 9: Skip first vertical bar, (TSS in next 5 vertical bars, tr lp around next dc lp or tr lp) across to last 6 vertical bars, TSS in last 6 vertical bars; work lps off hook.
Row 10: Skip first vertical bar, TSS in next 2 vertical bars, dc lp in next vertical bar on row before last, skip next vertical bar on last row, (TSS in next 2 vertical bars, dc-lp cluster around next tr lp, TSS in next 2 vertical bars, dc lp in next vertical bar on row before last, skip next vertical bar on last row) across to last 3 vertical bars, TSS in last 3 vertical bars; work lps off hook.
Pattern Rows: Repeat rows 5–10 consecutively to desired size, ending with row 6.
Next Row: Skip first vertical bar, TSS in next 2 vertical bars, dc-lp cluster around next tr lp, (TSS in next 5 vertical bars, dc-lp cluster around next tr lp) across to last 3 vertical bars, TSS in last 3 vertical bars; work lps off hook.
Next Two Rows: Work in TSS.
Last Row: Skip first vertical bar, insert hook in next vertical bar, yo, pull through 2 lps on hook *(sl st completed),* sl st in each vertical bar across. Fasten off.❑❑

MATERIALS

❑ Two desired colors of yarn (color A and color B)
❑ Easy Tunisian hook

SPECIAL STITCH

For **small puff stitch (sm puff st),** yo, insert hook from front to back between strands of next vertical bar on row before last, yo, pull up long lp, yo, insert hook in same sp, yo, pull up long lp, yo, pull through 4 lps on hook, ch 1.

NOTES

Read Tunisian Information on pages 1–4 before beginning pattern.

When changing colors (see illustration), carry dropped color loosely across ends of rows until needed.

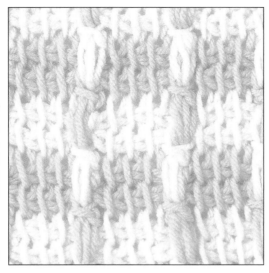

STITCH PATTERN

Row 1: With A, ch a minimum of 13 or in multiples of 4 plus 1, pull up lp in second ch from hook, pull up lp in each ch across, **do not turn;** work lps off hook.

Row 2: Work in TSS changing to B in last st made.

Row 3: Skip first vertical bar, TSS in next 3 vertical bars, **sm puff st** (see Special Stitch), (TSS in next 3 vertical bars, sm puff st) across to last 4 vertical bars, TSS in last 4 vertical bars; work lps off hook.

Row 4: Work in TSS changing to A in last st made.

Row 5: Skip first vertical bar, TSS in next 3 vertical bars, sm puff st, (TSS in next 3 vertical bars, sm puff st) across to last 4 vertical bars, TSS in last 4 vertical bars; work lps off hook.

Row 6: Work in TSS changing to B in last st made.

Pattern Rows: Repeat rows 3–6 consecutively to desired size, ending with row 5.

Last Row: Skip first vertical bar, insert hook in next vertical bar, yo, pull through 2 lps on hook (sl st completed), sl st in each vertical bar across. Fasten off.❑❑

MATERIALS
❑ Desired color yarn
❑ Easy Tunisian hook

SPECIAL STITCH
For **bobble,** yo, insert hook from front to back between strands of next vertical bar, yo, pull lp through, yo, pull through 2 lps on hook, *yo, insert hook in same sp, yo, pull lp through, yo, pull through 2 lps on hook; repeat from * one more time, yo, pull through 3 lps on hook, ch 1.

NOTE
Read Tunisian Information on pages 1–4 before beginning pattern.

STITCH PATTERN
Row 1: Ch a minimum of 15 or in multiples of 4 plus 3, pull up lp in second ch from hook, pull up lp in each ch across, **do not**

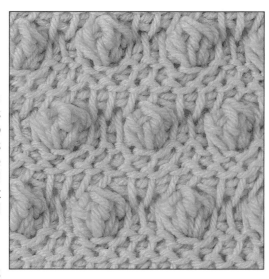

turn; work lps off hook.

Rows 2 & 3: Skip first vertical bar, work in TPS across to last vertical bar, TSS in last vertical bar; work lps off hook.

Row 4: Skip first vertical bar, TSS in next 2 vertical bars, **bobble** (see Special Stitch), TSS in next 3 vertical bars, (bobble, TSS in next 3 vertical bars) across; work lps off hook.

Rows 5 & 6: Skip first vertical bar, work in TPS across to last vertical bar, TSS in last vertical bar; work lps off hook.

Row 7: Skip first vertical bar, TSS in next 4 vertical bars, bobble, (TSS in next 3 vertical bars, bobble) across to last 5 vertical bars, TSS in last 5 vertical bars; work lps off hook.

Pattern Rows: Repeat rows 2–7 consecutively to desired size, ending with row 5.

Last Row: Skip first vertical bar; bring yarn to front of work, working behind yarn, insert hook in next vertical bar, yo, pull through 2 lps on hook (sl st completed), sl st in each vertical bar across. Fasten off.❑❑

2

Shell
Stitches

MATERIALS
- ❏ Desired color yarn
- ❏ Easy Tunisian hook

NOTE
Read Tunisian Information on pages 1–4 before beginning pattern.

STITCH PATTERN
Row 1: Ch a minimum of 8 or in multiples of 3 plus 2, pull up lp in second ch from hook, pull up lp in each ch across, **do not turn;** to **work lps off hook,** yo, pull through one lp on hook, ch 1, yo, pull through 4 lps on hook, (ch 2, yo, pull through 4 lps on hook—*this completes a shell and ch-3*) across to last 2 lps on hook, ch 1, yo, pull through last 2 lps on hook.

Row 2: Skip first vertical bar, pull up lp in next ch, skip next shell, (pull up lp in next 3 chs, skip next shell) across to last ch and vertical

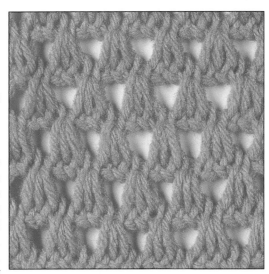

bar, pull up lp in next ch, pull up lp in last vertical bar *(ending with lps on hook in multiple of 3 plus 1);* to **work lps off hook,** yo, pull through one lp on hook, yo, pull through 2 lps on hook, (ch 2, yo, pull through 4 lps on hook) across

to last 3 lps on hook, ch 2, yo, pull through last 3 lps on hook.

Row 3: Ch 1, skip first vertical bar, pull up lp in next 3 chs, (skip next shell, pull up lp in next 3 chs) across to last vertical bar, pull up lp in last vertical bar *(ending with lps on hook in multiple of 3 plus 1);* to **work lps off hook,** yo, pull through one lp on hook, ch 1, yo, pull through 4 lps on hook, (ch 2, yo, pull through 4 lps on hook) across to last 2 lps on hook, ch 1, yo, pull through last 2 lps on hook.

Pattern Rows: Repeat rows 2 and 3 alternately to desired size.

Last Row: Using one size smaller hook, skip first vertical bar, (insert hook in next ch, yo, pull through 2 lps on hook—*sl st completed*) across skipping shells. Fasten off.❏❏

MATERIALS
❏ Desired color yarn
❏ Easy Tunisian hook

NOTE
Read Tunisian Information on pages 1–4 before beginning pattern.

STITCH PATTERN
Row 1: Ch a minimum of 8 or in multiples of 3 plus 2, pull up lp in second ch from hook, pull up lp in each ch across, **do not turn;** to **work lps off hook,** yo, pull through one lp on hook, ch 1, yo, pull through 4 lps on hook, (ch 2, yo, pull through 4 lps on hook—*this completes a shell and ch-3*) across to last 2 lps on hook, ch 1, yo, pull through last 2 lps on hook.

Row 2: Skip first vertical bar, pull up lp in ch before next shell, skip next shell, (pull up lp in next ch, insert hook in two strands of beginning ch on row 1 between vertical bars, yo, pull up long lp, ch 1, skip next ch on last row behind st just made, pull up lp in next ch, skip next shell) across to last ch sp and vertical bar, pull up lp in ch after next shell, insert hook in two strands of beginning ch between vertical bars, yo, pull up long lp, ch 1, pull up lp in last vertical bar; to **work lps off hook,** yo, pull through one lp on hook, yo, pull through 3 lps on hook *(half shell*

made), (ch 2, yo, pull through 4 lps on hook) across to last 3 lps on hook, ch 2, yo, pull through last 3 lps on hook.

Row 3: Ch 1, skip first vertical bar, pull up lp in next 3 chs, (skip next shell, pull up lp in next 3 chs) across to last half shell, skip next half shell, pull up lp in last vertical bar; to **work lps off hook,** yo, pull through one lp on hook, ch 1, yo, pull through 4 lps on hook, (ch 2, yo, pull through 4 lps on hook) across to last 2 lps on hook, ch 1, yo, pull through last 2 lps on hook.

Row 4: Skip first vertical bar, pull up lp in ch before next shell, skip next shell, (pull up lp in next ch, insert hook in two strands at top

of next shell on row before last, yo, pull up long lp, ch 1, skip next ch on last row behind st just made, pull up lp next ch, skip next shell) across to last ch sp and vertical bar, pull up lp in ch after next shell, insert hook in two strands at top of half shell on row before last, yo, pull up long lp, ch 1, pull up lp in last vertical bar; to **work lps off hook,** yo, pull through one lp on hook, yo, pull through 3 lps on hook *(half shell made),* (ch 2, yo, pull through 4 lps on hook) across to last 3 lps on hook, ch 2, yo, pull through last 3 lps on hook.

Pattern Rows: Repeat rows 3 and 4 alternately to desired size, ending with row 3.

Last Row: Skip first vertical bar, insert hook in next ch, yo, pull through 2 lps on hook *(sl st completed),* skip next shell, (sl st in next ch, insert hook in two strands at top of next shell on row before last, yo, pull up long lp, yo, pull through 2 lps on hook, skip next ch on last row behind st just made, sl st in next ch, skip next shell) across to last ch sp and vertical bar, sl st in next ch, insert hook in two strands at top of shell on row before last, yo, pull up long lp, yo, pull through 2 lps on hook, sl st in last vertical bar. Fasten off.❏❏

MATERIALS
❏ Desired color yarn
❏ Easy Tunisian hook

NOTE
Read Tunisian Information on pages 1–4 before beginning pattern.

STITCH PATTERN
Row 1: Ch a minimum of 7 or in multiples of 3 plus 1, pull up lp in second ch from hook, pull up lp in each ch across, **do not turn;** to **work lps off hook,** yo, pull through first 2 lps on hook *(first half shell made),* (ch 2, yo, pull through 4 lps on hook—*this completes a shell and ch-3*) across to last 3 lps on hook, ch 2, yo, pull through last 3 lps on hook *(last half shell completed).*

Row 2: Ch 1, (*pull up lp in next ch, insert hook in both strands of beginning ch on row 1 between shells, yo, pull up long lp, ch 1, skip next ch on last row behind st just made*, pull up lp in next ch, skip next shell) across to last ch sp and half shell; repeat between **, skip next ch, pull up lp in horizontal strand at top of last half shell; to **work lps off hook,** yo, pull through one lp on hook, yo, pull through 3 lps on hook, (ch 2, yo, pull through 4 lps on hook) across to last 2 lps on hook, ch 1, yo, pull through last 2 lps on hook.

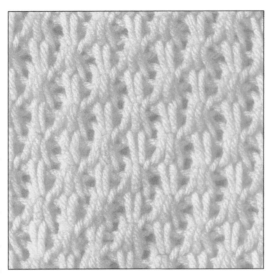

Row 3: Ch 1, skip first vertical bar, pull up lp in next ch, (skip next shell, pull up lp in next ch, insert hook in two strands of horizontal bar at top of next shell on row before last, yo, pull up long lp, ch 1, skip next ch on last row behind st just made, pull up lp in next ch) across to last half shell and vertical bar, pull up lp in horizontal bar at top of next half shell, pull up lp in last vertical bar; to **work lps off hook,** yo, pull through 2 lps on hook, (ch 2, yo, pull through 4 lps on hook) across to last 3 lps on hook, ch 2, yo, pull through last 3 lps on hook.

Row 4: Ch 1, (*pull up lp in next ch, insert hook in both strands of horizontal bar at top of next shell on row before last, yo, pull up long lp, ch 1, skip next ch on last row behind st just made*, pull up lp in next ch, skip next shell) across to last ch sp and half shell; repeat between **, skip next ch, pull up lp in horizontal strand at top of last half shell; to **work lps off hook,** yo, pull through one lp on hook, yo, pull through 3 lps on hook, (ch 2, yo, pull through 4 lps on hook) across to last 2 lps on hook, ch 1, yo, pull through last 2 lps on hook.

Pattern Rows: Repeat rows 3 and 4 alternately to desired size, ending with row 3.

Last Row: Ch 1, *[insert hook in next ch, yo, pull through 2 lps on hook *(sl st completed),* insert hook in both strands of horizontal bar at top of next shell on row before last, yo, pull up long lp, yo, pull through both lps on hook, skip next ch on last row behind st just made], sl st in next ch, skip next shell; repeat from * across to last ch sp and half shell; repeat between [ ], skip next ch, sl st in horizontal strand at top of last half shell. Fasten off.❏❏

MATERIALS
❏ Desired color yarn
❏ Easy Tunisian hook

NOTE
Read Tunisian Information on pages 1–4 before beginning pattern.

STITCH PATTERN
Row 1: Ch in multiples of 4 plus 1, pull up lp in second ch from hook, pull up lp in each ch across, **do not turn;** to **work lps off hook,** yo, pull through one lp on hook, (ch 1, yo, pull through 4 lps on hook—*ch-2 and shell made,* ch 1, yo, pull through 2 lps on hook) across.

Row 2: Skip first vertical bar,

(pull up lp in next ch sp, pull up lp in horizontal bar above

next shell, pull up lp in next ch sp, pull up lp in next vertical bar) across; to **work lps off hook,** yo, pull through one lp on hook, (ch 1, yo, pull through 4 lps on hook, ch 1, yo, pull through 2 lps on hook) across.

Pattern Row: Repeat row 2 to desired size.

Last Row: Skip first vertical bar, *insert hook in next ch sp, yo, pull through 2 lps on hook *(sl st completed),* sl st in horizontal bar above next shell, sl st in next ch sp, sl st in next vertical bar; repeat from * across. Fasten off.❏❏

MATERIALS
❏ Desired color yarn
❏ Easy Tunisian hook *(swatch in photo made with size L hook)*

NOTE
Read Tunisian Information on pages 1–4 before beginning pattern.

STITCH PATTERN
Row 1: Ch in multiples of 4 plus 2, pull up lp in third ch from hook, ch 1, (pull up lp in next ch, ch 1) across, **do not turn;** to **work lps off hook,** yo, pull through one lp on hook, (ch 1, yo, pull through 4 lps on hook—*ch-2 and shell made,* ch 1, yo, pull through 2 lps on hook) across.

Row 2: Ch 1, skip first vertical bar, (pull up lp in next ch sp,

ch 1, pull up lp in horizontal bar above next shell, ch 1, pull up lp in next ch sp, ch 1, pull up lp in next vertical bar, ch 1) across; to **work lps off hook,** yo, pull through one lp on hook, (ch 1, yo, pull through 4 lps on hook, ch 1, yo, pull through 2 lps on hook) across.

Pattern Row: Repeat row 2 to desired size.

Last Row: Ch 1, skip first vertical bar, *insert hook in next ch sp, yo, pull through 2 lps on hook *(sl st completed),* sl st in horizontal bar above next shell, sl st in next ch sp, sl st in next vertical bar; repeat from * across. Fasten off.❏❏

MATERIALS
❑ Desired color yarn
❑ Easy Tunisian hook

NOTE
Read Tunisian Information on pages 1–4 before beginning pattern.

STITCH PATTERN
Row 1: Ch a minimum of 9 or in multiples of 4 plus 1, pull up lp in second ch from hook, pull up lp in each ch across, **do not turn;** to **work lps off hook,** yo, pull through one lp on hook, (ch 1, yo, pull through 4 lps on hook—*ch-2 and shell made,* ch 1, yo, pull through 2 lps on hook) across.

Row 2: Skip first vertical bar, (pull up lp in ch before next shell, pull up lp in horizontal bar at top of next shell, pull up lp in ch after same shell, pull up lp in next vertical bar) across; to **work lps off hook,** yo, pull through one lp on hook, ch 1, yo, pull through 2 lps on hook, ch 1, yo, pull through 4 lps on hook, (ch 1, yo, pull through 2 lps on hook, ch 1, yo, pull through 4 lps on

hook) across.

Row 3: Ch 1, skip first shell, pull up lp in ch after same shell, pull up lp in next vertical bar, (pull up lp in ch before next shell, pull up lp in horizontal bar at top of next shell, pull up lp in ch after same shell, pull up lp in next vertical bar) across to last ch sp and vertical bar, pull up lp in next ch, pull up lp in last vertical bar; to **work lps off hook,** yo, pull through one lp on hook, (yo, pull

through 2 lps on hook) 3 times, (ch 1, yo, pull through 4 lps on hook, ch 1, yo, pull through 2 lps on hook) across to last 2 lps on hook, yo, pull through last 2 lps on hook.

Row 4: Skip first vertical bar, pull up lp in next vertical bar, (pull up lp in ch before next shell, pull up lp in horizontal bar at top of next shell, pull up lp in next ch after same shell, pull up lp in next vertical bar) across to last 3 vertical bars, pull up lp in each of last 3 vertical bars; to **work lps off hook,** yo, pull through one lp on hook, (ch 1, yo, pull through 4 lps on hook, ch 1, yo, pull through 2 lps on hook) across.

Pattern Rows: Repeat rows 2–4 consecutively to desired size.

Last Row: Skip first vertical bar, *insert hook in ch before next shell, yo, pull through 2 lps on hook *(sl st completed),* sl st in horizontal bar at top of next shell, sl st in ch after same shell, sl st in next vertical bar; repeat from * across. Fasten off.❑❑

MATERIALS
❑ Desired color yarn
❑ Easy Tunisian hook

NOTE
Read Tunisian Information on pages 1–4 before beginning pattern.

STITCH PATTERN
Row 1: Ch a minimum of 7 or in multiples of 3 plus 1, pull up lp in second ch from hook, pull up lp in each ch across, **do not turn;** to **work lps off hook,** yo, pull through 2 lps on hook *(first half shell made),* (ch 2, yo, pull through 4 lps on hook—*ch-3 and shell made)* across to last 3 lps on hook, ch 2, yo, pull through last 3 lps on hook *(last half shell made).*

Row 2: Ch 1, skip first shell, (*pull up lp in next ch, insert hook in one strand of beginning ch on row 1 between shells, skip next ch on last row behind st just made*, pull up lp in next ch, skip next shell) across to last ch sp and half shell; repeat between **, pull up lp in horizontal bar at top of last half shell; to **work lps off hook,** yo, pull through one lp on hook, ch 1, yo, pull through 3 lps on hook *(half shell made),* (ch 2, yo, pull through 4 lps on hook) across to

last 2 lps on hook, ch 1, yo, pull through last 2 lps on hook.

Row 3: Ch 1, skip first vertical bar, pull up lp in ch before next shell, (skip next shell, pull up lp in next ch, insert hook in horizontal strand at top of next shell on row before last, yo, pull up long lp, skip next ch on last row behind st just made, pull up lp in next ch) across to half shell, skip next half shell, pull up lp in next ch, pull up lp in last vertical bar; to **work lps off hook,** yo, pull through 2 lps on hook *(half shell made),* (ch 2, yo, pull through 4 lps on hook) across to last 3 lps on hook,

ch 2, yo, pull through last 3 lps on hook *(half shell made).*

Row 4: Ch 1, skip first shell, (*pull up lp in next ch, insert hook in top horizontal strand at top of next shell on row before last, yo, pull up long lp, skip next ch on last row behind st just made*, pull up lp in next ch, skip next shell) across to last ch sp and half shell; repeat between **, pull up lp in horizontal bar at top of last half shell; to **work lps off hook,** yo, pull through one lp on hook, ch 1, yo, pull through 3 lps on hook *(half shell made),* (ch 2, yo, pull through 4 lps on hook) across to last 2 lps on hook, ch 1, yo, pull through last 2 lps on hook.

Pattern Rows: Repeat rows 3 and 4 alternately to desired size, ending with row 3.

Last Row: Ch 1, skip first shell, (*insert hook in next ch, yo, pull through 2 lps on hook—*sl st completed,* sl st in top horizontal strand at top of next shell on row before last, skip next ch on last row behind st just made*, sl st in next ch, skip next shell) across to last ch sp and half shell; repeat between **, sl st in horizontal bar at top of last half shell. Fasten off.❑❑

MATERIALS
❑ Desired color yarn
❑ Easy Tunisian hook

NOTE
Read Tunisian Information on pages 1–4 before beginning pattern.

STITCH PATTERN
Row 1: Ch a minimum of 13 or in multiples of 5 plus 3, pull up lp in third ch from hook, ch 1, (pull up lp in next ch, ch 1) across, **do not turn; to work lps off hook,** yo, pull through one lp on hook, ch 2, yo, pull through 6 lps on hook *(ch-3 and shell made)*, (ch 4, yo, pull through 6 lps on hook—*ch-5 and shell made)* across to last 2 lps on hook, ch 1, yo, pull through last 2 lps on hook.

Row 2: Ch 1, skip first vertical bar, (pull up lp in next ch, ch 1) 2 times, skip next shell, *(pull up lp in next ch, ch 1) 5 times, skip next shell; repeat from * across to

last ch sp, (pull up lp in next ch, ch 1) 3 times; to **work lps off hook,** yo, pull through one lp on hook, yo, pull through 3 lps on hook *(half shell made)*, (ch 4, yo, pull through 6 lps on hook) across to last 4 lps on hook, ch 4, yo, pull through last 4 lps on hook *(half shell made)*.

Row 3: Ch 1, skip first shell, (pull up lp in next ch, ch 1) 5 times, *skip next shell, (pull up lp in next ch, ch 1) 5 times; repeat from * across to last half shell and ch sp, skip next half shell, pull up lp in last ch; to **work lps off hook,** yo, pull through one lp on hook, ch 2, yo, pull through 6 lps on hook *(ch-3 and shell made)*, (ch 4, yo, pull through 6 lps on hook—*ch-5 and shell made)* across to last 2 lps on hook, ch 1, yo, pull through last 2 lps on hook.

Pattern Rows: Repeat rows 2 and 3 alternately to desired size.

Last Row: Ch 1, skip first vertical bar, (insert hook in next ch, yo, pull through 2 lps on hook—*sl st completed,* ch 1) 2 times, skip next shell, *(sl st in next ch, ch 1) 5 times, skip next shell; repeat from * across to last ch sp, sl st in next ch, (ch 1, sl st in next ch) 2 times. Fasten off.❑❑

MATERIALS
❑ Desired color yarn
❑ Easy Tunisian hook

NOTE
Read Tunisian Information on pages 1–4 before beginning pattern.

STITCH PATTERN
Row 1: Ch a minimum of 12 or in multiples of 5 plus 2, pull up lp in second ch from hook, pull up lp in each ch across, **do not turn; to work lps off hook,** yo, pull through one lp on hook, ch 1, yo, pull through 6 lps on hook *(ch-2 and shell made)*, (ch 3, yo, pull through 6 lps on hook—*ch-4 and shell made)* across to last 2 lps on hook, ch 1, yo, pull through last 2 lps on hook.

Row 2: Skip first vertical bar, pull up lp in next 2 chs, pull up lp in horizontal bar at top of next shell, (pull up lp in next 4 chs, pull up lp in horizontal bar at top

of next shell) across to last ch sp and vertical bar, pull up lp in next 2 chs, pull up lp in last vertical bar; to **work lps off hook,** yo, pull through one lp on hook, ch 1, yo, pull through 6 lps on hook, (ch 4, yo, pull through 6 lps on hook) across to last 2 lps on hook, ch 1, yo, pull through last 2 lps on hook.

Pattern Row: Repeat row 2 to desired size.

Last Row: Skip first vertical bar, insert hook in next ch, yo, pull through 2 lps on hook *(sl st completed)*, sl st in each ch and in horizontal bar at top of each shell across. Fasten off.❑❑

MATERIALS
❑ Desired color yarn
❑ Easy Tunisian hook

NOTE
Read Tunisian Information on pages 1–4 before beginning pattern.

STITCH PATTERN
Row 1: Ch in multiples of 3 plus 2, pull up lp in second ch from hook, pull up lp in each ch across, **do not turn;** to **work lps off hook,** yo, pull through one lp on hook, (ch 1, yo, pull through 4 lps on hook—*ch-2 and shell made*) across to last 2 lps on hook, ch 1, yo, pull through last 2 lps on hook.

Row 2: Skip first vertical bar, pull

up lp in ch before next shell, pull up lp in horizontal bar at top of

next shell, (pull up lp in next 2 chs, pull up lp in horizontal bar at top of next shell) across to last ch sp and vertical bar, pull up lp in next ch, pull up lp in last vertical bar; to **work lps off hook,** yo, pull through one lp on hook, (ch 1, yo, pull through 4 lps on hook) across to last 2 lps on hook, ch 1, yo, pull through last 2 lps on hook.

Pattern Row: Repeat row 2 to desired size.

Last Row: Skip first vertical bar, insert hook in next ch, yo, pull through 2 lps on hook *(sl st completed)*, sl st in horizontal bar at top of each shell and in each ch across. Fasten off.❑❑

MATERIALS
❑ Desired color yarn
❑ Easy Tunisian hook

NOTE
Read Tunisian Information on pages 1–4 before beginning pattern.

STITCH PATTERN
Row 1: Ch in multiples of 10 plus 7, pull up lp in second ch from hook, pull up lp in each ch across, **do not turn; to work lps off hook,** yo, pull through one lp on hook, ch 1, yo, pull through 6 lps on hook *(ch-2 and shell made),* *ch 1, (yo, pull through 2 lps on hook) 5 times, ch 1, yo, pull through 6 lps on hook; repeat from * across to last 2 lps on hook, ch 1, yo, pull through last 2 lps on hook.

Row 2: Skip first vertical bar, (*pull up lp in next 2 chs, pull up lp in horizontal bar at top of next shell, pull up lp in next 2 chs*, pull up lp in next 5 vertical bars) across to last 2 ch sps and shell;

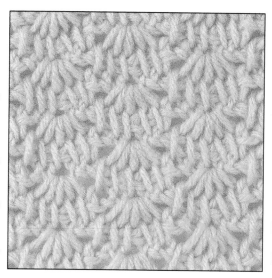

repeat between **, pull up lp in last vertical bar; to **work lps off hook,** yo, pull through one lp on hook, *(yo, pull through 2 lps on hook) 5 times, ch 1, yo, pull through 6 lps on hook, ch 1; repeat from * across to last 7 lps on hook, (yo, pull through 2 lps on hook) 6 times.

Row 3: Skip first vertical bar, (pull up lp in next 5 vertical bars, pull

up lp in next 2 chs, pull up lp in horizontal bar at top of next shell, pull up lp in next 2 chs) across to last 6 vertical bars, pull up lp in last 6 vertical bars; to **work lps off hook,** yo, pull through one lp on hook, ch 1, yo, pull through 6 lps on hook, *ch 1, (yo, pull through 2 lps on hook) 5 times, ch 1, yo, pull through 6 lps on hook; repeat from * across to last 2 lps on hook, ch 1, yo, pull through last 2 lps on hook.

Pattern Rows: Repeat rows 2 and 3 to desired size.

Last Row: Skip first vertical bar, insert hook in next ch, yo, pull through 2 lps on hook *(sl st completed),* sl st in next ch, sl st in horizontal bar at top of next shell, sl st in next 2 chs, (sl st in next 5 vertical bars, sl st in next 2 chs, sl st in horizontal bar at top of next shell, sl st in next 2 chs) across to last vertical bar, sl st in last vertical bar. Fasten off.❑❑

MATERIALS
❏ Two desired colors of yarn (color A and color B)
❏ Easy Tunisian hook

NOTES
Read Tunisian Information on pages 1–4 before beginning pattern.

When changing colors (see illustration), carry dropped color loosely across ends of rows until needed.

STITCH PATTERN
Row 1: With A, ch a minimum of 12 or in multiples of 5 plus 2, pull up lp in second ch from hook, pull up lp in each ch across, **do not turn;** to **work lps off hook,** yo, pull through one lp on hook, ch 1, yo, pull through 6 lps on hook (ch-2 and shell made), (ch 4, yo, pull through 6 lps on hook—ch-5 and shell made) across to last 2 lps on hook, ch 1, yo, pull through last 2 lps on hook changing to B.

Row 2: Ch 1, skip first vertical bar, insert hook in beginning ch on row 1 before next shell, yo, pull up long lp, ch 1, skip next ch on last row behind st just made, pull up lp in ch before next shell, skip next shell, (pull up lp in next 2 chs, insert hook in beginning ch on row 1 between next 2 shells, yo, pull up long lp, ch 1, skip next ch on last row behind st just made, pull up lp in next 2 chs, skip next shell) across to last ch sp and vertical bar, pull up lp in next ch, insert hook in beginning ch on row 1 between next 2 shells, yo, pull up long lp, ch 1, skip next ch on last row behind st just made, pull up lp in last vertical bar (ending with lps on hook in multiples of 5 plus 1); to **work lps off hook,** yo, pull through one lp on hook, yo, pull through 3 lps on hook (half shell made), (ch 4, yo, pull through 6 lps on hook) across to last 4 lps on hook, ch 4, yo, pull through last 4 lps on hook (half shell made) changing to A.

Row 3: Ch 1, skip first shell, (*pull up lp in next 2 chs, insert hook in two horizontal strands of next shell on row before last, yo, pull up long lp, ch 1, skip next ch on last row behind st just made, pull up lp in next 2 chs*, skip next shell) across to last ch sp and half shell; repeat between **, skip next half shell, pull up lp in last vertical bar (ending with lps on hook in multiples of 5 plus 2); to **work lps off hook,** yo, pull through one lp on hook, ch 2, yo, pull through 6 lps on hook, (ch 4, yo, pull through 6 lps on hook) across to last 2 lps on hook, ch 1, yo, pull through last 2 lps on hook changing to B.

Row 4: Ch 1, skip first vertical bar, insert hook in two horizontal strands of next shell on row before last, yo, pull up long lp, ch 1, skip next ch on last row behind st just made, pull up lp in ch before next shell, skip next shell, (pull up lp in next 2 chs, insert hook in two horizontal strands of next shell on row before last, yo, pull up long lp, ch 1, skip next ch on last row behind st just made, pull up lp in next 2 chs, skip next shell) across to last ch sp and vertical bar, pull up lp in next ch, insert hook in two horizontal strands of next shell on row before last, yo, pull up long lp, ch 1, skip next ch on last row behind st just made, pull up lp in last vertical bar (ending with lps on hook in multiples of 5 plus 1); to **work lps off hook,** yo, pull through one lp on hook, yo, pull through 3 lps on hook, (ch 4, yo, pull through 6 lps on hook) across to last 4 lps on hook, ch 4, yo, pull through last 4 lps on hook changing to A.

Pattern Rows: Repeat rows 3 and 4 to desired size, ending with row 3.

Last Row: With B, ch 1, skip first vertical bar, insert hook in two horizontal strands of next shell on row before last, yo, pull through 2 lps on hook (sl st completed), sl st in ch before next shell, skip next shell, (sl st in next 2 chs, sl st in two horizontal strands of next shell on row before last, sl st in next 2 chs, skip next shell) across to last ch sp and vertical bar, sl st in next ch, sl st in two horizontal strands of next shell on row before last, sl st in last vertical bar. Fasten off.❏❏

MATERIALS
❑ Desired color yarn
❑ Easy Tunisian hook

SPECIAL STITCH
For **limpet shell,** *hold the yarn with the left hand and wrap clockwise around left index finger; scoop the hook under the yarn from front to back toward the fingertip (see photo), and lift the yarn off your finger to form a loop on the hook, pull the yarn snug; move the right index finger over the last loop made to hold it in place; repeat from * 7 more times, yo, pull through 8 lps on hook, insert hook in next vertical bar, yo, pull lp through bar and one lp on hook.

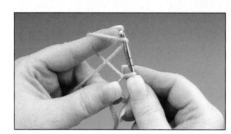

NOTE
Read Tunisian Information on pages 1–4 before beginning pattern.

STITCH PATTERN
Row 1: Ch the desired number, pull up lp in second ch from hook, pull up lp in each ch across, **do not turn;** work lps off hook.

Pattern Rows: Work in TSS across to where shell is desired, work **limpet shell** (see Special Stitch), complete row in TSS. You may work shells where desired. Continue to desired size.

Last Row: Skip first vertical bar, *insert hook in next vertical bar, yo, pull through 2 lps on hook (sl st completed), sl st in each vertical bar across. Fasten off.❑❑

MATERIALS
❑ Desired color yarn
❑ Easy Tunisian hook

SPECIAL STITCH
For **double crochet loop (dc lp),** yo, insert hook in specified st, yo, pull lp through, yo, pull through 2 lps on hook.

NOTE
Read Tunisian Information on pages 1–4 before beginning pattern.

STITCH PATTERN
Row 1: Ch in multiples of 3 plus 2, pull up lp in second ch from hook, pull up lp in each ch across, **do not turn; to work lps off hook,** yo, pull through one lp on hook, ch 1, yo, pull through 4 lps on hook (ch-2 and shell made), (ch 2, yo, pull through 4 lps on

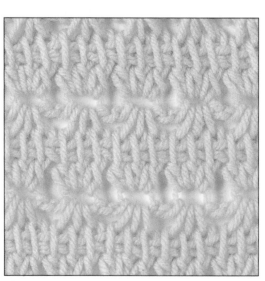

hook—ch-3 and shell made) across to last 2 lps on hook, ch 1, yo, pull through last 2 lps on hook.

Row 2: Ch 1, skip first vertical bar, 3 **dc lps** (see Special Stitch) in horizontal bar at top of next

shell, 3 dc lps in horizontal bar at top of each shell across to last vertical bar, TSS in last vertical bar; to **work lps off hook,** yo, pull through one lp on hook, (yo, pull through 2 lps on hook) across.

Row 3: Skip first vertical bar, TSS in each vertical bar across; to **work lps off hook,** yo, pull through one lp on hook, ch 1, yo, pull through 4 lps on hook, (ch 2, yo, pull through 4 lps on hook) across to last 2 lps on hook, ch 1, yo, pull through last 2 lps on hook.

Pattern Rows: Repeat rows 2 and 3 alternately to desired size.

Last Row: Ch 1, skip first vertical bar, pull up lp in next ch, yo, pull through 2 lps on hook (sl st completed), sl st in horizontal bar of each shell and in each ch across. Fasten off.❑❑

Openwork Patterns

3

MATERIALS
- ❑ Desired color yarn
- ❑ Easy Tunisian hook

NOTE
Read Tunisian Information on pages 1–4 before beginning pattern.

STITCH PATTERN
Row 1: Ch a minimum of 11 or in multiples of 4 plus 3, pull up lp in second ch from hook, pull up lp in each ch across, **do not turn;** work lps off hook.

Row 2: Skip first vertical bar, (yo, skip next vertical bar, TSS in next vertical bar) across; work lps off hook.

Row 3: Skip first vertical bar, (pull up

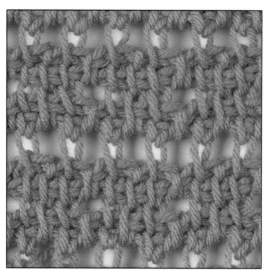

lp in next ch sp, TSS in next vertical bar) across; work lps off hook.

Row 4: Skip first vertical bar, TSS in next 2 vertical bars, (yo, skip next vertical bar, TSS in next 3 vertical bars) across; work lps off hook.

Row 5: Skip first vertical bar, TSS in next 2 vertical bars, (pull up lp in next ch sp, TSS in next 3 vertical bars) across; work lps off hook.

Pattern Rows: Repeat rows 2–5 consecutively to desired size, ending with row 3.

Last Row: Skip first vertical bar, insert hook in next vertical bar, yo, pull through 2 lps on hook *(sl st completed),* sl st in each vertical bar across. Fasten off.❑❑

MATERIALS
- ❑ Desired color yarn
- ❑ Easy Tunisian hook

NOTE
Read Tunisian Information on pages 1–4 before beginning pattern.

STITCH PATTERN
Row 1: Ch a minimum of 7 or in multiples of 3 plus 1, pull up lp in second ch from hook, pull up lp in each ch across, **do not turn;** work lps off hook.

Row 2: Skip first vertical bar, (yo, skip next vertical bar, TSS in next

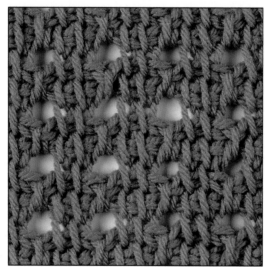

2 vertical bars) across; work lps off hook.

Row 3: Skip first vertical bar, (pull up lp in next ch sp, TSS in next 2 vertical bars) across; work lps off hook.

Pattern Rows: Repeat rows 2 and 3 alternately to desired size, ending with row 2.

Last Row: Skip first vertical bar, insert hook in next ch sp, yo, pull lp through, yo, pull through 2 lps on hook *(sc completed),* sl st in each vertical bar and sc in each ch sp across. Fasten off.❑❑

MATERIALS
❑ Desired color yarn
❑ Easy Tunisian hook

NOTE
Read Tunisian Information on pages 1–4 before beginning pattern.

STITCH PATTERN
Row 1: Ch a minimum of 7 or in multiples of 2 plus 1, pull up lp in second ch from hook, pull up lp in each ch across, **do not turn;** work lps off hook.

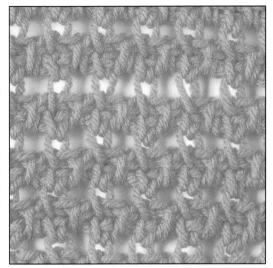

Row 2: Skip first vertical bar, TSS in next vertical bar, (yo, skip next vertical bar, TSS in next vertical bar) across to last vertical bar, TSS in last vertical bar; work lps off hook.

Row 3: Work in TSS.

Pattern Rows: Repeat rows 2 and 3 alternately to desired size.

Last Row: Skip first vertical bar, insert hook in next vertical bar, yo, pull through 2 lps on hook *(sl st completed)*, sl st in each vertical bar across. Fasten off.❑❑

MATERIALS
❑ Desired color yarn
❑ Easy Tunisian hook

NOTE
Read Tunisian Information on pages 1–4 before beginning pattern.

STITCH PATTERN
Row 1: Ch in multiples of 6 plus 3, pull up lp in second ch from hook, pull up lp in each ch across, **do not turn;** work lps off hook.

Row 2: Skip first vertical bar, TSS in

next 2 vertical bars, *yo, skip next vertical bar, TSS in next vertical bar, yo, skip next vertical bar, TSS in next 3 vertical bars; repeat from * across; work lps off hook.

Pattern Rows: Repeat row 2 to desired size.

Last Row: Skip first vertical bar, insert hook in next vertical bar, yo, pull through 2 lps on hook *(sl st completed)*, sl st in each vertical bar and sc in each ch sp across. Fasten off.❑❑

MATERIALS
❑ Desired color yarn
❑ Easy Tunisian hook

NOTE
Read Tunisian Information on pages 1–4 before beginning pattern.

STITCH PATTERN
Row 1: Ch in multiples of 2, pull up lp in second ch from hook, pull up lp in each ch across, **do not turn;** work lps off hook.

Row 2: Skip first vertical bar, (pull up lp in next 2 vertical bars at same time, yo) across to last verti-

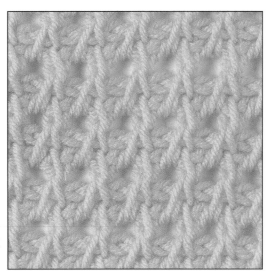

cal bar, pull up lp in last vertical bar; work lps off hook.

Row 3: Skip first vertical bar, pull up lp in next vertical bar, (pull up lp in next ch sp, pull up lp in next vertical bar) across; work lps off hook.

Pattern Rows: Repeat rows 2 and 3 alternately to desired size, ending with row 2.

Last Row: Skip first vertical bar, insert hook in next vertical bar, yo, pull through 2 lps on hook *(sl st completed),* sl st in each ch sp and in each vertical bar across. Fasten off.❑❑

MATERIALS
❑ Desired color yarn
❑ Easy Tunisian hook

NOTE
Read Tunisian Information on pages 1–4 before beginning pattern.

STITCH PATTERN
Row 1: Ch in multiples of 4 plus 3, pull up lp in second ch from hook, pull up lp in each ch across, **do not turn;** work lps off hook.

Row 2: Skip first vertical bar, TSS in next 2 vertical bars, (yo, skip next vertical bar, TSS in next 3

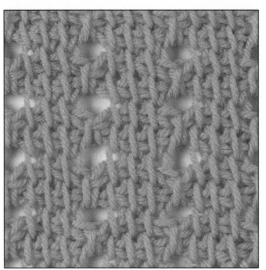

vertical bars) across; work lps off hook.

Row 3: Skip first vertical bar, TSS in next 2 vertical bars, (pull up lp in next ch sp, TSS in next 3 vertical bars) across; work lps off hook.

Pattern Rows: Repeat rows 2 and 3 alternately to desired size, ending with row 2.

Last Row: Skip first vertical bar, insert hook in next vertical bar, yo, pull through 2 lps on hook *(sl st completed),* sl st in next vertical bar, (sc in next ch sp, sl st in next 3 vertical bars) across. Fasten off.❑❑

MATERIALS
❑ Desired color yarn
❑ Easy Tunisian hook

SPECIAL STITCH
For **double crochet loop (dc lp)**, yo, insert hook in specified st, yo, pull lp through, yo, pull through 2 lps on hook.

NOTE
Read Tunisian Information on pages 1–4 before beginning pattern.

STITCH PATTERN
Row 1: Ch in multiples of 2, pull up lp in second ch from hook, pull up lp in each ch across, **do not turn;** work lps off hook.

Row 2: Ch 1, skip first 2 vertical bars, **dc lp** *(see Special Stitch)* in next vertical bar; working in front of last st made, dc lp in second skipped vertical bar, (skip next vertical bar, dc lp in next vertical bar; working in front of last st made, dc lp in skipped vertical bar) across to last vertical bar, pull up lp in last vertical bar; work lps off hook.

Row 3: Work in TSS.

Pattern Rows: Repeat rows 2 and 3 alternately to desired size, ending with row 2.

Last Row: Skip first vertical bar, insert hook in next vertical bar, yo, pull through 2 lps on hook *(sl st completed),* sl st in each vertical bar across. Fasten off.❑❑

MATERIALS
❑ Desired color yarn
❑ Easy Tunisian hook

NOTE
Read Tunisian Information on pages 1–4 before beginning pattern.

STITCH PATTERN
Row 1: Ch in multiples of 4 plus 3, pull up lp in second ch from hook, pull up lp in each ch across, **do not turn;** work lps off hook.

Rows 2 & 3: Skip first vertical bar, TSS in next 2 vertical bars, (yo, skip next vertical bar or next ch

sp, TSS in next 3 vertical bars) across; work lps off hook.

Row 4: Skip first vertical bar, TSS in next 2 vertical bars; (working over last row, insert hook in ch sp on row before last, yo, pull up long lp, TSS in next 3 vertical bars) across; work lps off hook.

Pattern Rows: Repeat rows 2–4 consecutively to desired size, ending with row 2.

Last Row: Skip first vertical bar, insert hook in next vertical bar, yo, pull through 2 lps on hook *(sl st completed),* sl st in each vertical bar and in each ch sp across. Fasten off.❑❑

MATERIALS
❑ Desired color yarn
❑ Easy Tunisian hook

NOTE
Read Tunisian Information on pages 1–4 before beginning pattern.

STITCH PATTERN
Row 1: Ch a minimum of 31 or in multiples of 12 plus 7, pull up lp in second ch from hook, pull up lp in each ch across, **do not turn;** work lps off hook.

Row 2: Skip first vertical bar, TSS in next 8 vertical bars, yo, skip next vertical bar, (TSS in next 11 vertical bars, yo, skip next vertical bar) across to last 9 vertical bars; TSS in next 9 vertical bars; work lps off hook.

Row 3: Skip first vertical bar, TSS in next 6 vertical bars, yo, skip next vertical bar, TSS in next 3 vertical bars, yo, skip next vertical

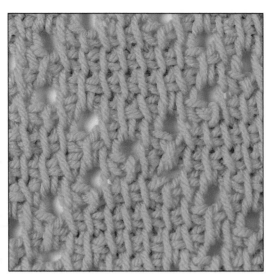

bar, (TSS in next 7 vertical bars, yo, skip next vertical bar, TSS in next 3 vertical bars, yo, skip next vertical bar) across to last 7 vertical bars; TSS in last 7 vertical bars; work lps off hook.

Row 4: Skip first vertical bar, TSS in next 4 vertical bars, yo, skip next vertical bar, TSS in next 7 vertical bars, yo, skip next vertical bar, (TSS in next 3 vertical bars, yo, skip next vertical bar, TSS in next 7 vertical bars, yo, skip next vertical bar) across to last 5 vertical bars; TSS in last 5 vertical bars; work lps off hook.

Row 5: Skip first vertical bar, TSS in next 2 vertical bars, yo, skip next vertical bar, (TSS in next 11 vertical bars, yo, skip next vertical bar) across to last 3 vertical bars; TSS in last 3 vertical bars; work lps off hook.

Row 6: Repeat row 4.

Row 7: Repeat row 3.

Pattern Rows: Repeat rows 2–7 consecutively to desired size, ending with row 2.

Next Row: Work in TSS.

Last Row: Skip first vertical bar, insert hook in next vertical bar, yo, pull through 2 lps on hook (*sl st completed*), sl st in each vertical bar across. Fasten off.❑❑

4

Cable
& Post
Stitches

MATERIALS
❑ Desired color yarn
❑ Easy Tunisian hook

NOTE
Read Tunisian Information on pages 1–4 before beginning pattern.

STITCH PATTERN
Row 1: Ch 19 (*this stitch pattern requires 4 sts for each "cable" plus the number of sts you desire between cables*), pull up lp in second ch from hook, pull up lp in each ch across, **do not turn;** work lps off hook.

Rows 2 & 3: Work in TSS.

Row 4: Skip first vertical bar, TSS in next 7 vertical bars, skip next vertical bar on row before last, tr around both bars of next vertical

bar, TSS in next 4 vertical bars on last row; working behind last tr completed, tr around both bars of same vertical bar, TSS in last

7 vertical bars on last row; work lps off hook.

Row 5: Work in TSS.

Row 6: Skip first vertical bar, TSS in next 7 vertical bars, tr around both bars of vertical bar centered between tr on row before last, TSS in next 4 vertical bars on last row; working behind last tr made, tr around both bars of same vertical bar, TSS in last 7 vertical bars on last row; work lps off hook.

Pattern Rows: Repeat rows 5 and 6 alternately to desired size.

Last Row: Skip first vertical bar, insert hook in next vertical bar, yo, pull through 2 lps on hook (*sl st completed*), sl st in each vertical bar across. Fasten off.❑❑

MATERIALS
❑ Desired color yarn
❑ Easy Tunisian hook

NOTE
Read Tunisian Information on pages 1–4 before beginning pattern.

STITCH PATTERN
Row 1: Ch a minimum of 14 or in multiples of 6 plus 2, pull up lp in second ch from hook, pull up lp in each ch across, **do not turn;** work lps off hook.

Rows 2 & 3: Work in TSS.

Row 4: Skip first vertical bar, TSS in next 2 vertical bars, (*skip next vertical bar 3 rows below, tr around both bars of next vertical bar, TSS in next 2 vertical bars on last row; working behind last tr made, tr around both bars of

same vertical bar*, TSS in next 4 vertical bars on last row) across to last 5 vertical bars; repeat between **, TSS in last 3 vertical bars on last row; work lps off hook.

Row 5: Work in TSS.

Row 6: Skip first vertical bar, TSS in next 2 vertical bars, (*tr around both bars of next vertical bar centered between tr 3 rows below, TSS in next 2 vertical bars on last row; working behind last tr made, tr around both bars of same vertical bar*, TSS in next 4 vertical bars on last row) across to last 5 vertical bars; repeat between **, TSS in last 3 vertical bars; work lps off hook.

Pattern Rows: Repeat rows 5 and 6 alternately to desired size.

Last Row: Skip first vertical bar, insert hook in next vertical bar, yo, pull through 2 lps on hook (*sl st completed*), sl st in each vertical bar across. Fasten off.❑❑

BEADED PURSE

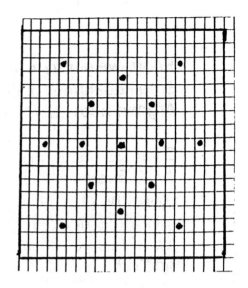

MATERIALS:

1 x 50 grm. ball of sports weight
        or DK yarn
1 x 4.50 afghan hook
1 x 3.50 crochet hook
15 beads

FRONT:

With 4,50 afghan hook make a chain of 17 stitches
Work 2 rows in basic Tunisian crochet
Starting on row 3 of chart, (1 square = there _and_ back, reading
from right to left), incorporate beads into work as indicated..
When 21 rows are completed, bind off

BACK:

Make a chain of 17 stitches
Work 21 rows in basic Tunisian crochet
Bind off

ASSEMBLY:

With 3.50 ___ ook work 1 double crochet in each stitch across
top of ___ fasten off
Place ___ her, wrong sides together
Wit ___ double crochet through both
t ___ bottom and up third side,
___ off.
W ___ ke a chain 22 ins. Long;
sew ___

___re Fantastics, 2003

MOUSE COASTER

Sportsweight yarn in main colour
Small quantities of brown, pink and black
Afghan hook size 4.50 mm.

Chain 25 sts. in main colour
Work 6 rows
Following chart, complete next 8 rows, using bobbins of different colours as needed
Work 7 rows in main colour
Bind off

Optional: using 3.50 crochet hook, work a row of single crochet around coaster, placing 3 sts. in each corner

Press with damp cloth

☐ Main colour
▣ Brown
◪ Pink
▦ —— Black embroidery

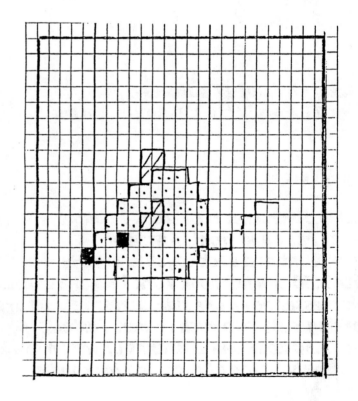

Julia Bryant, Fibre Fantastics, 2002

TUNISIAN CROCHET SAMPLER

Materials: 4.50 mm. afghan crochet hook
DK/sports weight yarn in 2 colours
10 beads
small piece of plastic canvas 3" x 1'

BEFORE STARTING WORK, THREAD 5 BEADS ON BOTH COLOUR A AND COLOUR B YARNS

Chain 15 stitches with colour A
Work 15 rows in colour A
Following chart, starting at row 16, place
   colours, beads and bobbles as indicated.
Bind off

Assembly:
Turn under top 3 rows, and hem in place
   to make a facing. Insert strip of plastic
   canvas, hem ends closed.
Crochet a 12 chain loop, and sew in centre of
   top.
At lower end, turn ends back to form a point,
   and hem into place.
Add tassel.

Press lightly with a damp cloth.

Julia Bryant, Fibre Fantastics, 2006

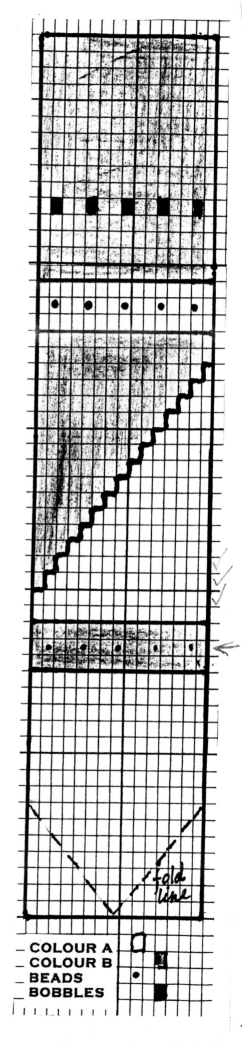

COLOUR A
COLOUR B
BEADS
BOBBLES

Tunisian Crochet

Tunisian or Afghan crochet is worked with a long hook available in the same range of thicknesses as traditional crochet hooks. The hooks are longer than crochet hooks as they are required to hold the loops created on the first (Forward) half of the row before working them off on the return half.

The fabric produced by this technique can be dense and thick. It is important to use a suitable size of hook in relation to the yarn. This is usually at least two sizes larger than would be used when working ordinary crochet with the same yarn.

Each row is worked in two parts. The first or 'Forward' part of the row involves working from right to left and pulling up loops or stitches on to the hook. On the second or 'Return' part of the row these loops are worked off again as the hook travels back from left to right. Tunisian crochet is nearly always made without turning, therefore the right side is always facing.

Holding the Hook

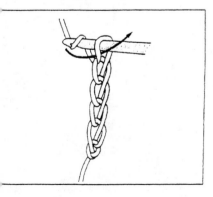

The hook should be held in the centre with the hand as shown in the diagram.

Starting Chain

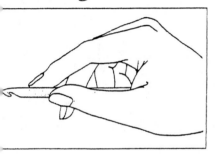

Make the number of chains needed to correspond with the number of stitches required in the first row.

Tip

When working a large piece it is sensible to start with more chains than necessary as it is simple to undo the extra chains if you have miscounted.

Although there are exceptions, Tunisian stitch patterns usually begin with the same initial forward and return row - referred to as: **Basic Forward and Return row.**

Forward

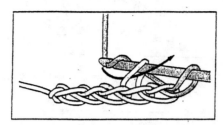

1. Working into back loop only of each chain, insert hook into second chain from hook, yarn over, draw loop through and leave on hook.

2. Insert hook into next chain, yarn over, draw loop through and leave on hook.

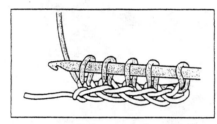

Repeat this in each chain to end. Do not turn.

The number of loops on hook should equal the number of stitches required for first row.

Note: Because the fabric produced in Tunisian crochet is usually firmer than in ordinary crochet we recommend that the hook is inserted into the back loop only of the starting chain as this produces a firmer edge.

Return

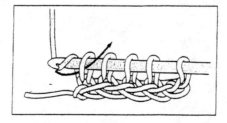

1. Yarn over, draw through one loop. (This chain forms the edge stitch).

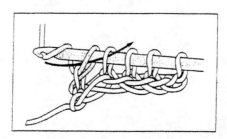

2. Yarn over, and draw through two loops.

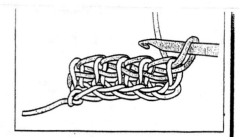

3. Repeat step 2 until one loop remains on hook. Do not turn. The loop remaining on the hook becomes the first stitch of the following row.

The Basic Stitches

These are produced by varying the technique of picking up loops on the Forward row.

Tunisian Simple Stitch (Tss ⍭)

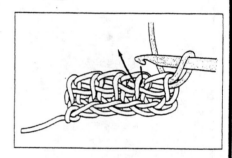

1. Insert hook from right to left behind single vertical thread.

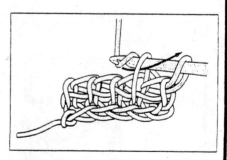

2. Yarn over hook.

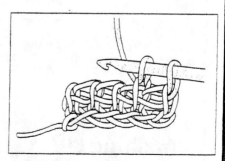

3. Draw loop through and leave on hook.

Unless otherwise stated, the hook is always inserted in this way. For example, Tunisian half trebles, trebles etc. are usually worked from this position.

Making Tunisian Fabric

Make chain as required and work a Basic Forward and Return row. Generally the single loop on the hook at the end of each Return row counts as the first stitch in the next Forward row and so the first stitch is missed. (As shown in first diagram for Tunisian simple stitch).

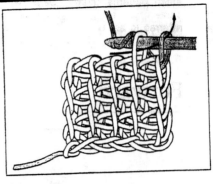

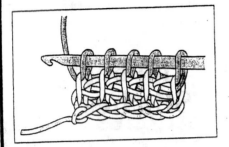

Next row: Pick up loop in each stitch (Tss or as required) including edge stitch.

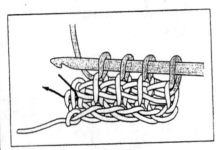

If you require a firmer edge at this end of the row you can work through two loops of the last stitch.
Return as Basic Return row.

1. Finish with Return row. Insert hook into next stitch, yarn over.

2. Draw through two loops.
Repeat steps 1 and 2 to end. Fasten off remaining loop.

BOOK SOURCE;
Harmony Guide to 100's More Crochet Stitches
1992 Lyric Books Limited

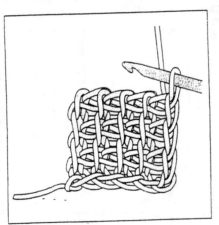

Repeat Forward and Return row as required. It is important to understand how to produce basic Tunisian fabric before attempting pattern stitches.

Finishing Off

It is possible simply to finish with a Return row, cutting yarn and threading it through the remaining stitch to secure. However the following method leaves a neater edge and is useful where the Tunisian fabric is complete in itself - as for a mat or rug for example.

MATERIALS
❑ Desired color yarn
❑ Easy Tunisian hook

NOTE
Read Tunisian Information on pages 1–4 before beginning pattern.

STITCH PATTERN
Row 1: Ch 19 *(this stitch pattern requires 4 sts for each "cable" plus the number of sts you desire between cables)*, pull up lp in second ch from hook, pull up lp in each ch across, **do not turn;** work lps off hook.

Rows 2–6: Work in TSS.

Row 7: Skip first vertical bar, TSS in next 7 vertical bars, skip next vertical bar 3 rows below, tr around both strands of next vertical bar, TSS in next 2 vertical

bars on last row; working in front of last tr, tr around both bars of same vertical bar 3 rows below, TSS in next 2 vertical bars on last row; working behind last 2

tr, tr around both bars of same vertical bar 3 rows below, TSS in last 7 vertical bars on last row; work lps off hook.

Rows 8 & 9: Work in TSS.

Row 10: Skip first vertical bar, TSS in next 7 vertical bars, tr around post of next tr 3 rows below, (TSS in next 2 vertical bars on last row, tr around post of next tr 3 rows below) 2 times, TSS in last 7 vertical bars on last row; work lps off hook.

Rows 11 & 12: Work in TSS.

Pattern Rows: Repeat rows 7–12 consecutively to desired size.

Last Row: Skip first vertical bar, insert hook in next vertical bar, yo, pull through 2 lps on hook *(sl st completed)*, sl st in each vertical bar across. Fasten off.❑❑

MATERIALS
- ❏ Desired color yarn
- ❏ Easy Tunisian hook

NOTE
Read Tunisian Information on pages 1–4 before beginning pattern.

SPECIAL STITCH
For **treble loop (tr lp),** yo 2 times, insert hook in specified st, yo, pull lp through, (yo, pull through 2 lps on hook) 2 times.

STITCH PATTERN
Row 1: Ch 19 *(this stitch pattern requires 5 sts for each "diamond" plus the number of sts you desire between diamonds),* pull up lp in second ch from hook, pull up lp in each ch across, **do not turn;** work lps off hook.

Rows 2 & 3: Work in TSS.

Row 4: Skip first vertical bar, TSS in next 8 vertical bars, **tr lp** *(see Special Stitch)* around both strands of next vertical bar on row before last, skip next vertical bar on last

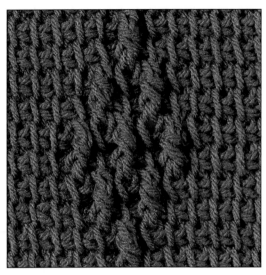

row behind tr lp, TSS in last 9 vertical bars; work lps off hook.

Row 5: Work in TSS.

Row 6: Skip first vertical bar, TSS in next 7 vertical bars, tr lp around both strands of next vertical bar on row before last, skip next vertical bar on last row behind tr lp, TSS in next vertical bar, tr lp around both strands of next vertical bar on row before last,

skip next vertical bar on last row behind tr lp, TSS in last 8 vertical bars; work lps off hook.

Row 7: Work in TSS.

Row 8: Skip first vertical bar, TSS in next 6 vertical bars, tr lp around both strands of next vertical bar on row before last, skip next vertical bar on last row behind tr lp, (TSS in next vertical bar, tr lp around both strands of next vertical bar on row before last, skip next vertical bar on last row behind tr lp) 2 times, TSS in last 7 vertical bars; work lps off hook.

Row 9: Work in TSS.

Row 10: Repeat row 6.

Row 11: Work in TSS.

Row 12: Repeat row 4.

Row 13: Work in TSS.

Pattern Rows: Repeat rows 4–13 consecutively to desired size.

Last Row: Skip first vertical bar, insert hook in next vertical bar, yo, pull through 2 lps on hook *(sl st completed),* sl st in each vertical bar across. Fasten off.❏❏

MATERIALS
- ❑ Desired color yarn
- ❑ Easy Tunisian hook

NOTE
Read Tunisian Information on pages 1–4 before beginning pattern.

STITCH PATTERN
Row 1: Ch 19 *(this stitch pattern requires 7 sts for each "cable pattern" plus the number of sts you desire between patterns)*, pull up lp in second ch from hook, pull up lp in each ch across, **do not turn;** work lps off hook.

Rows 2–4: Work in TSS.

Row 5: Skip first vertical bar, TSS in next 9 vertical bars, tr around both strands of seventh vertical bar 3 rows below, tr around

both strands of tenth vertical bar 4 rows below, skip next 5 vertical bars after first tr 3 rows below, tr around both strands

of next vertical bar, TSS in last 9 vertical bars on last row; work lps off hook.

Rows 6 & 7: Work in TSS.

Row 8: Skip first vertical bar, TSS in next 9 vertical bars, tr around both strands of seventh vertical bar 3 rows below, (skip next 2 vertical bars on same row, tr around both strands of next vertical bar) 2 times, TSS in last 9 vertical bars on last row; work lps off hook.

Pattern Rows: Repeat rows 6–8 consecutively to desired size, ending with row 7.

Last Row: Skip first vertical bar, insert hook in next vertical bar, yo, pull through 2 lps on hook *(sl st completed)*, sl st in each vertical bar across. Fasten off.❑❑

MATERIALS
- ❑ Desired color yarn
- ❑ Easy Tunisian hook

NOTE
Read Tunisian Information on pages 1–4 before beginning pattern.

STITCH PATTERN
Row 1: Ch 19 *(this stitch pattern requires 4 sts for each "V" pattern plus the number of sts you want between patterns)*, pull up lp in second ch from hook, pull up lp in each ch across, **do not turn;** work lps off hook.

Rows 2 & 3: Work in TSS.

Row 4: Skip first vertical bar, TSS in next 3 vertical bars, (*skip next vertical bar on row before last, tr around both strands of next vertical bar on row before last, TSS in

next 4 vertical bars on last row; working behind last tr, tr around both strands of same vertical bar on row before last*, TSS in next 4 vertical bars on last row; repeat

between **, TSS in last 3 vertical bars; work lps off hook.

Rows 5 & 6: Work in TSS.

Row 7: Skip first vertical bar, TSS in next 7 vertical bars, skip next vertical bar on row before last, tr around both strands of next vertical bar on row before last, TSS in next 4 vertical bars on last row; working behind last tr, tr around both strands of same vertical bar on row before last, TSS in last 7 vertical bars on last row; work lps off hook.

Rows 8 & 9: Work in TSS.

Pattern Rows: Repeat rows 4–9 consecutively to desired size.

Last Row: Skip first vertical bar, insert hook in next vertical bar, yo, pull through 2 lps on hook *(sl st completed)*, sl st in each vertical bar across. Fasten off.❑❑

MATERIALS
❑ Desired color yarn
❑ Easy Tunisian hook

SPECIAL STITCH
For **puff stitch (puff st),** yo, insert hook from front to back between both strands of next vertical bar, yo, pull up lp, (yo, insert hook from front to back in same sp, yo, pull up lp) 2 times, yo, pull through 6 lps on hook.

NOTE
Read Tunisian Information on pages 1–4 before beginning pattern.

STITCH PATTERN
Row 1: Ch a minimum of 19 or in multiples of 8 plus 3, pull up lp in second ch from hook, pull up lp in each ch across, **do not turn;** work lps off hook.
Rows 2 & 3: Work in TSS.
Row 4: Skip first vertical bar, TSS in

next 3 vertical bars, *skip next vertical bar on row before last, tr around both strands of next vertical bar on row before last, TSS in next 4 vertical bars on last row; working behind last tr, tr around both strands of same vertical bar on row before last*, TSS in next 4 vertical bars on last row;

repeat between **, TSS in last 3 vertical bars; work lps off hook.
Rows 5 & 6: Work in TSS.
Row 7: Skip first vertical bar, TSS in next 5 vertical bars, (tr around next tr 3 rows below) 2 times, tr around next tr on row before last, TSS in next 8 vertical bars on last row, tr around each of next 2 tr on row before last, TSS in last 5 vertical bars; work lps off hook.
Row 8: Work in TSS.
Row 9: Skip first vertical bar, TSS in next 4 vertical bars, **puff st** *(see Special Stitch),* TSS in next 7 vertical bars, puff st, TSS in last 5 vertical bars; work lps off hook.
Pattern Rows: Repeat rows 2–9 consecutively to desired size, ending with row 8.
Last Row: Skip first vertical bar, insert hook in next vertical bar, yo, pull through 2 lps on hook *(sl st completed),* sl st in each vertical bar across. Fasten off.❑❑

MATERIALS
❑ Desired color yarn
❑ Easy Tunisian hook

SPECIAL STITCH
For **extended single crochet (esc),** yo, insert hook around both lps at the base of designated vertical bar, yo, pull lp through, yo, pull through one lp on hook, yo, pull through 2 lps on hook.

NOTE
Read Tunisian Information on pages 1–4 before beginning pattern.

STITCH PATTERN
Row 1: Ch in multiples of 2 plus 1, pull up lp in second ch from hook,

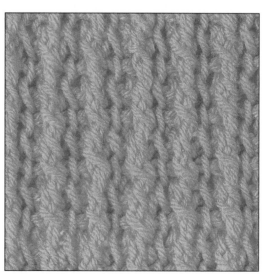

pull up lp in each ch across, **do not turn;** work lps off hook.

Row 2: Work in TSS.
Row 3: Skip first vertical bar, **esc** *(see Special Stitch)* around next vertical bar on row before last, skip next vertical bar on last row, TSS in next vertical bar, (esc around next vertical bar on row before last, skip next vertical bar on last row, TSS in next vertical bar) across; work lps off hook.
Pattern Rows: Repeat rows 2 and 3 alternately to desired size, ending with row 3.
Last Row: Skip first vertical bar, insert hook in next vertical bar, yo, pull through 2 lps on hook *(sl st completed),* sl st in each vertical bar across. Fasten off.❑❑

MATERIALS
- ❏ Desired color yarn
- ❏ Easy Tunisian hook

NOTE
Read Tunisian Information on pages 1–4 before beginning pattern.

STITCH PATTERN
Row 1: Ch a minimum of 15 or in multiples of 6 plus 3, pull up lp in second ch from hook, pull up lp in each ch across, **do not turn;** work lps off hook.

Row 2: Skip first vertical bar, TSS in next 6 vertical bars, yo, skip next vertical bar, (TSS in next 5 vertical bars, yo, skip next vertical bar) across to last 7 vertical bars, TSS in last 7 vertical bars; work lps off hook.

Row 3: Skip first vertical bar, TSS in each vertical bar and in each ch sp across; work lps off hook.

Row 4: Skip first vertical bar, TSS in next 3 vertical bars, (*tr around

both strands of fifth vertical bar 3 rows below, TSS in next 2 vertical bars on last row; working behind tr just made, tr around same vertical bar 3 rows below*, TSS in next vertical bar on last row, yo, skip next vertical bar, TSS in next 2 vertical bars) across to last 5 vertical bars; repeat between **,

TSS in last 3 vertical bars on last row; work lps off hook.

Row 5: Repeat row 3.

Row 6: Repeat row 2.

Row 7: Skip first vertical bar, TSS in next 3 vertical bars, (*tr around both strands of vertical bar centered between tr 3 rows below, TSS in next 2 vertical bars on last row; working behind tr just made, tr around same vertical bar 3 rows below*, TSS in next vertical bar on last row, pull up lp in next ch sp, TSS in next 2 vertical bars) across to last 5 vertical bars; repeat between **, TSS in last 3 vertical bars on last row; work lps off hook.

Pattern Rows: Repeat rows 2–7 consecutively to desired size.

Last Row: Skip first vertical bar, insert hook in next vertical bar, yo, pull through 2 lps on hook *(sl st completed),* sl st in each vertical bar across. Fasten off.❏❏

MATERIALS
❏ Desired color yarn
❏ Easy Tunisian hook

NOTE
Read Tunisian Information on pages 1–4 before beginning pattern.

STITCH PATTERN
Row 1: Ch the desired number, pull up lp in second ch from hook, pull up lp in each ch across, **do not turn;** work lps off hook.

Row 2: Skip first vertical bar, TSS in each vertical bar across; to **work lps off hook,** yo, pull through one lp on hook, *(yo, pull through 2 lps on hook) across to where ch lp is desired, ch 8; repeat from * if desired for more ch lps, (yo, pull through 2 lps on hook) across.

Rows 3 & 4: Work in TSS.

Row 5: Skip first vertical bar, TSS in each vertical bar across; to **work lps off hook,** yo, pull through one lp on hook, *(yo, pull through 2 lps on hook) across to ch lp 3 rows below, ch 8; repeat from * if applicable, (yo, pull through 2 lps on hook) across.

Pattern Rows: Repeat rows 3–5 consecutively, ending with row 4. At end of last row, to **lace ch lps,** pull second lp through first lp, pull third lp through second lp, continue in this manner until all lps are laced.

Next Row: Skip first vertical bar, *TSS in each vertical bar across to ch lp below, insert hook in next ch lp, yo, pull lp through, skip next vertical bar on last row; repeat from * if applicable, TSS in each vertical bar across; work lps off hook.

Last Row: Skip first vertical bar, insert hook in next vertical bar, yo, pull through 2 lps on hook (sl st completed), sl st in each vertical bar across. Fasten off.❏❏

MATERIALS
❏ Desired color yarn
❏ Easy Tunisian hook

NOTE
Read Tunisian Information on pages 1–4 before beginning pattern.

STITCH PATTERN
Row 1: Ch 21 (cable/post st pattern requires 7 sts plus desired number of sts on each side), pull up lp in second ch from hook, pull up lp in each ch across, **do not turn;** work lps off hook.

Rows 2–7: Work in TSS.

Row 8: Skip first vertical bar, TSS in next 10 vertical bars, tr around both strands of eighth vertical bar 3 rows below, (skip next 2

vertical bars 3 rows below, tr around both strands of next vertical bar) 2 times, TSS in last 10 vertical bars on last row; work lps off hook.

Rows 9 & 10: Work in TSS.

Row 11: Skip first vertical bar, TSS in next 7 vertical bars, tr around both vertical strands at top of next 3-tr group 3 rows below, (TSS in next 3 vertical bars on last row; working behind last tr, tr in same sp as last tr) 2 times, TSS in last 7 vertical bars on last row; work lps off hook.

Rows 12 & 13: Work in TSS.

Pattern Rows: Repeat rows 8–13 consecutively to desired size.

Next Row: Work in TSS.

Last Row: Skip first vertical bar, insert hook in next vertical bar, yo, pull through 2 lps on hook (sl st completed), sl st in each vertical bar across. Fasten off.❏❏

MATERIALS
- ❏ Two desired colors of yarn (*color A and color B*)
- ❏ Easy Tunisian hook

SPECIAL STITCH
For **double crochet lp (dc lp),** yo, insert hook around designated st, yo, pull lp through, yo, pull through one lp on hook, yo, pull through 2 lps on hook. Skip next vertical bar on last row behind dc lp.

NOTES
Read Tunisian Information on pages 1–4 before beginning pattern.

When changing colors (*see illustration*), carry dropped color loosely across ends of rows until needed.

STITCH PATTERN
Row 1: With A, ch in multiples of 3, pull up lp in second ch from hook, pull up lp in each ch across, **do not turn;** work lps off hook.

Row 2: Work in TSS changing to B in last st made.

Row 3: Skip first vertical bar, **dc lp** (*see Special Stitch*) around both strands of next vertical bar on row before last, (TSS in next 2 vertical bars on last row, dc lp around both strands of next vertical bar on row before last) across to last vertical bar on last row, TSS in last vertical bar; work lps off hook.

Row 4: Work in TSS, changing to A in last st made.

Row 5: Skip first vertical bar, dc lp around both strands of next vertical bar on row before last, (TSS in next 2 vertical bars on last row, dc lp around both strands of next vertical bar on row before last) across to last vertical bar on last row, TSS in last vertical bar; work lps off hook.

Pattern Rows: Repeat rows 2–5 consecutively to desired size.

Last Row: Skip first vertical bar, insert hook in next vertical bar, yo, pull through 2 lps on hook (*sl st completed*), sl st in each vertical bar across. Fasten off.❏❏

MATERIALS
- ❏ Desired color yarn
- ❏ Easy Tunisian hook

NOTE
Read Tunisian Information on pages 1–4 before beginning pattern.

STITCH PATTERN
Row 1: Ch a minimum of 19 or in multiples of 8 plus 3, pull up lp in second ch from hook, pull up lp in each ch across, **do not turn;** work lps off hook.

Rows 2 & 3: Work in TSS.

Row 4: Skip first vertical bar, TSS in next 3 vertical bars, (*skip next vertical bar 3 rows below, tr around next vertical bar 3 rows below, TSS in next 4 vertical bars

on last row; working behind first tr, tr around same vertical bar 3 rows below*, TSS in next 4 vertical bars on last row) across to last 7 vertical bars; repeat between **, TSS in last 3 vertical bars; work lps off hook.

Rows 5 & 6: Work in TSS.

Row 7: Skip first vertical bar, TSS in next 5 vertical bars, (tr around next tr 3 rows below) 2 times, *TSS in next 8 vertical bars, (tr around next tr 3 rows below) 2 times; repeat from * across to last 5 vertical bars, TSS in last 5 vertical bars; work lps off hook.

Pattern Rows: Repeat rows 2–7 consecutively to desired size.

Last Row: Skip first vertical bar, insert hook in next vertical bar, yo, pull through 2 lps on hook (*sl st completed*), sl st in each vertical bar across. Fasten off.❏❏

MATERIALS
❑ Desired color yarn
❑ Easy Tunisian hook

SPECIAL STITCHES
For **double treble crochet lp (dtr lp),** yo 3 times, insert hook around post of specified st, yo, pull lp through, (yo, pull through 2 lps on hook) 3 times. Skip next vertical bar on last row behind dtr.

For **bobble,** yo, insert hook from front to back between strands of next vertical bar, yo, pull lp through, yo, pull through 2 lps on hook, *yo, insert hook in same sp, yo, pull lp through, yo, pull through 2 lps on hook; repeat from * one more time, yo, pull through 3 lps on hook, ch 1.

NOTE
Read Tunisian Information on pages 1–4 before beginning pattern.

STITCH PATTERN
Row 1: Ch a minimum of 19 or in multiples of 8 plus 3, pull up lp in second ch from hook, pull up lp in each ch across, **do not turn;** work lps off hook.

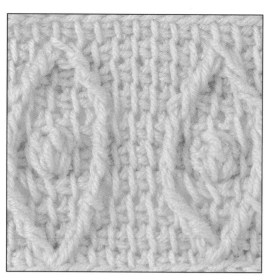

Rows 2 & 3: Work in TSS.
Row 4: Skip first vertical bar, TSS in next 2 vertical bars, skip first 5 vertical bars 3 rows below, ***dtr lp (s**ee Special Stitches) around both strands of next vertical bar 3 rows below, TSS in next 3 vertical bars; working behind last dtr, dtr lp around same vertical bar 3 rows below, TSS in next 3 vertical bars*, [skip next 7 vertical bars 3 rows below; repeat between **]; repeat between [ ] across if applicable; work lps off hook.
Row 5: Work in TSS.

Row 6: Skip first vertical bar, TSS in next 4 vertical bars, **bobble** *(see Special Stitches),* (TSS in next 7 vertical bars, bobble) across to last 5 vertical bars, TSS in last 5 vertical bars; work lps off hook.
Row 7: Skip first vertical bar, TSS in next 2 vertical bars, (dtr lp around post of dtr 3 rows below, TSS in next 3 vertical bars) across; work lps off hook.
Row 8: Work in TSS.
Row 9: Skip first vertical bar, TSS in next 4 vertical bars, (dtr lp around post of dtr 3 rows below) 2 times, skip next vertical bar on last row behind 2 dtr, TSS in next 7 vertical bars, (dtr lp around post of dtr 3 rows below) 2 times, skip next vertical bar on last row behind 2 dtr, TSS in last 5 vertical bars; work lps off hook.
Rows 10–12: Work in TSS.
Pattern Rows: Repeat rows 4–12 consecutively to desired size, ending with row 9.
Last Row: Skip first vertical bar, insert hook in next vertical bar, yo, pull through 2 lps on hook *(sl st completed),* sl st in each vertical bar across. Fasten off.❑❑

MATERIALS
❑ Desired color yarn
❑ Easy Tunisian hook

SPECIAL STITCHES
For **double treble crochet lp (dtr lp),** yo 3 times, insert hook around post of specified st, yo, pull lp through, (yo, pull through 2 lps on hook) 3 times. Skip next vertical bar on last row behind dtr lp.

For **treble crochet lp (tr lp),** yo 2 times, insert hook around post of specified st, yo, pull lp through, (yo, pull through 2 lps on hook) 2 times. Skip next vertical bar on last row behind tr lp.

For **bobble,** yo, insert hook around both strands of specified vertical bar, yo, pull lp through, yo, pull through 2 lps on hook, *yo, insert hook in same sp, yo, pull lp through, yo, pull through 2 lps on hook; repeat from * one more time, yo, pull through 3 lps on hook, ch 1.

NOTE
Read Tunisian Information on pages 1–4 before beginning pattern.

STITCH PATTERN
Row 1: Ch in multiples of 6 plus 3, pull up lp in second ch from hook, pull up lp in each ch across, **do not turn;** work lps off hook.

Row 2: Work in TSS.

Row 3: Skip first vertical bar, TSS in next 2 vertical bars, *skip next 2 vertical bars on row before last, **dtr lp** (see Special Stitches) around both strands of next vertical bar; working behind dtr just made, TSS in second skipped vertical bar; working in front of dtr, dtr lp around both strands of first skipped vertical bar, TSS in next 3 vertical bars; repeat from * across; work lps off hook.

Row 4: Work in TSS.

Row 5: Skip first vertical bar, TSS in next 2 vertical bars, *tr lp (see Special Stitches) around post of next dtr, **bobble** (see Special Stitches) around both strands of next vertical bar on row before last (between dtr), skip next vertical bar on last row, tr lp around post of next dtr, TSS in next 3 vertical bars; repeat from * across; work lps off hook.

Row 6: Work in TSS.

Row 7: Skip first vertical bar, TSS in next 2 vertical bars, *skip next tr lp and bobble on row before last, dtr lp around post of next tr lp; working behind dtr just made, TSS in next st; working in front of dtr lp, dtr lp around post of first skipped tr lp, TSS in next 3 vertical bars; repeat from * across; work lps off hook.

Pattern Rows: Repeat rows 4–7 consecutively to desired size.

Last Row: Skip first vertical bar, insert hook in next vertical bar, yo, pull through 2 lps on hook (sl st completed), sl st in each vertical bar across. Fasten off.❑❑

MATERIALS
❑ Desired color yarn
❑ Easy Tunisian hook

SPECIAL STITCHES
For **treble crochet lp (tr lp),** yo 2 times, insert hook around post of specified st, yo, pull lp through, (yo, pull through 2 lps on hook) 2 times. Skip next vertical bar on last row behind tr lp.

For **double treble crochet lp (dtr lp),** yo 3 times, insert hook around post of specified st, yo, pull lp through, (yo, pull through 2 lps on hook) 3 times. Skip next vertical bar on last row behind dtr lp.

NOTE
Read Tunisian Information on pages 1–4 before beginning pattern.

STITCH PATTERN
Row 1: Ch in multiples of 6 plus 3, pull up lp in second ch from hook, pull up lp in each ch across, **do not turn;** work lps off hook.

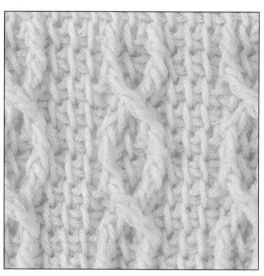

Rows 2 & 3: Work in TSS.
Row 4: Skip first vertical bar, TSS in next 2 vertical bars, *tr lp (see Special Stitches)* around both strands of next vertical bar 3 rows below, TSS in next vertical bar on last row, tr lp around next vertical bar 3 rows below, TSS in next 3 vertical bars on last row; repeat from * across; work lps off hook.
Row 5: Work in TSS.

Row 6: Skip first vertical bar, TSS in next 2 vertical bars, *skip next 2 vertical bars, **dtr lp** (see Special Stitches) around post of next tr on row before last; working behind dtr just made, TSS in second skipped vertical bar on last row; working in front of dtr, dtr lp around post of first skipped tr on row before last, TSS in next 3 vertical bars on last row; repeat from * across; work lps off hook.
Row 7: Work in TSS.
Row 8: Skip first vertical bar, TSS in next 2 vertical bars, (tr lp around next dtr on row before last, TSS in next vertical bar on last row, tr lp around next dtr on row before last, TSS in next 3 vertical bars on last row) across; work lps off hook.
Pattern Rows: Repeat rows 5–8 consecutively to desired size, ending with row 8.
Last Row: Skip first vertical bar, insert hook in next vertical bar, yo, pull through 2 lps on hook *(sl st completed),* sl st in each vertical bar across. Fasten off.❑❑

5

Pattern
Stitches

MATERIALS
❑ Desired color yarn
❑ Easy Tunisian hook

NOTE
Read Tunisian Information on pages 1–4 before beginning pattern.

STITCH PATTERN
Row 1: Ch desired number, pull up lp in second ch from hook, pull

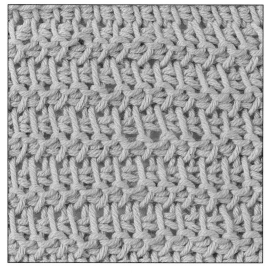

up lp in each ch across, **do not turn;** work lps off hook.
Row 2: Work in TPS.
Row 3: Work in TSS.
Pattern Rows: Repeat rows 2 and 3 alternately to desired size.
Last Row: Skip first vertical bar, insert hook in next vertical bar, yo, pull through 2 lps on hook (*sl st completed*), sl st in each vertical bar across. Fasten off.❑❑

MATERIALS
❑ Desired color yarn
❑ Easy Tunisian hook

NOTE
Read Tunisian Information on pages 1–4 before beginning pattern.

STITCH PATTERN
Row 1: Ch 19 (*center TRS stitch pattern requires 7 sts plus number of sts you desire between each TRS stitch pattern*), pull up lp in second ch from hook, pull up lp in each ch across, **do not turn;** work lps off hook.
Rows 2–5: Work in TSS.
Row 6: Skip first vertical bar, TSS in next 7 vertical bars, (insert hook through work from back to front between strands of next vertical bar—*TRS completed*) 3 times, TSS

in last 8 vertical bars; work lps off hook.
Row 7: Skip first vertical bar, TSS in next 6 vertical bars, TRS in next 2 vertical bars, TSS in next vertical

bar, TRS in next 2 vertical bars, TSS in next 7 vertical bars; work lps off hook.
Rows 8 & 9: Skip first vertical bar, TSS in next 5 vertical bars, TRS in next 2 vertical bars, TSS in next 3 vertical bars, TRS in next 2 vertical bars, TSS in last 6 vertical bars; work lps off hook.
Row 10: Repeat row 7.
Row 11: Repeat row 6.
Rows 12–15: Work in TSS.
Pattern Rows: Repeat rows 6–15 consecutively to desired size.
Last Row: Skip first vertical bar, insert hook in next vertical bar, yo, pull through 2 lps on hook (*sl st completed*), sl st in each vertical bar across. Fasten off.❑❑

MATERIALS
❑ Desired color yarn
❑ Easy Tunisian hook

NOTE
Read Tunisian Information on pages 1–4 before beginning pattern.

STITCH PATTERN
Row 1: Ch in multiples of 3 plus 2, pull up lp in second ch from hook, pull up lp in each ch across, **do not turn;** work lps off hook.

Row 2: Skip first vertical bar, *insert hook in next 3 vertical bars at same time, yo, pull lp through, TSS in center vertical bar of 3-bar group

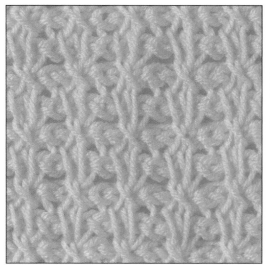

just formed, TSS in first bar of same 3-bar group; repeat from * across to last vertical bar, TSS in last vertical bar; work lps off hook.

Row 3: Work in TSS.

Pattern Rows: Repeat rows 2 and 3 alternately to desired size.

Last Row: Skip first vertical bar, *insert hook in next 3 vertical bars at same time, yo, pull lp through bars and lp on hook *(sl st completed),* sl st in center vertical bar of 3-bar group just formed, sl st in first bar of same 3-bar group; repeat from * across to last vertical bar, sl st in last vertical bar. Fasten off.❑❑

MATERIALS
❑ Desired color yarn
❑ Easy Tunisian hook

NOTE
Read Tunisian Information on pages 1–4 before beginning pattern.

STITCH PATTERN
Row 1: Ch a minimum of 6 or in multiples of 2, pull up lp in second ch from hook, pull up lp in each ch across, **do not turn;** work lps off hook.

Row 2: Skip first vertical bar, (insert hook in next 2 vertical bars at same time, yo, pull lp through, TSS in first vertical bar of 2-bar groups just formed) across to last vertical bar, TSS in last vertical bar; work lps off hook.

Row 3: Skip first vertical bar, TSS in next vertical bar, (insert hook in next 2 vertical bars at same time, yo, pull lp through, TSS in first

vertical bar of 2-bar groups just formed) across to last 2 vertical bars, TSS in last 2 vertical bars; work lps off hook.

Pattern Rows: Repeat rows 2 and 3 alternately to desired size, ending with row 2.

Last Row: Skip first vertical bar, insert hook in next vertical bar, yo, pull through 2 lps on hook *(sl st completed),* (sl st in next 2 vertical bars at same time, sl st in first vertical bar of 2-bar groups just formed) across to last 2 vertical bars, sl st in last 2 vertical bars. Fasten off.❑❑

No. 64

MATERIALS
❑ Desired color yarn
❑ Easy Tunisian hook

NOTE
Read Tunisian Information on pages 1–4 before beginning pattern.

STITCH PATTERN
Row 1: Ch a minimum of 6 or in multiples of 2, pull up lp in second ch from hook, pull up lp in each ch across, **do not turn;** work lps off hook.

Row 2: Skip first vertical bar, (insert hook in next 2 vertical bars at same time, yo, pull lp through, TSS in first vertical bar of 2-bar group just formed) across to last vertical bar, TSS

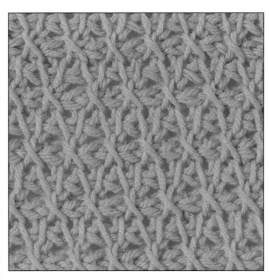

in last vertical bar; work lps off hook.

Row 3: Work in TSS.

Row 4: Skip first vertical bar, TSS in next vertical bar, (insert hook in next 2 vertical bars at same time, yo, pull lp through, TSS in first vertical bar of 2-bar group just formed) across to last 2 vertical bars, TSS in last 2 vertical bars; work lps off hook.

Row 5: Work in TSS.

Pattern Rows: Repeat rows 2–5 consecutively to desired size, ending with row 3.

Last Row: Skip first vertical bar, insert hook in next vertical bar, yo, pull through 2 lps on hook *(sl st completed)*, (sl st in next 2 vertical bars at same time, yo, pull lp through, sl st in first vertical bar of 2-bar group just formed) across to last 2 vertical bars, sl st in last 2 vertical bars. Fasten off.❑❑

No. 65

MATERIALS
❑ Desired color yarn
❑ Easy Tunisian hook

NOTE
Read Tunisian Information on pages 1–4 before beginning pattern.

STITCH PATTERN
Row 1: Ch in multiples of 6, pull up lp in second ch from hook, pull up lp in each ch across, **do not turn;** work lps off hook.

Row 2: Skip first vertical bar, TSS in next 4 vertical bars, TPS in next vertical bar, (TSS in next 5 vertical bars, TPS in next vertical bar) across; work lps off hook.

Row 3: Skip first vertical bar, TSS in next 3 vertical bars, TPS in next 2 vertical bars, (TSS in next 4 vertical

bars, TPS in next 2 vertical bars) across; work lps off hook.

Row 4: Skip first vertical bar, TSS in next 2 vertical bars, TPS in next 3

vertical bars, (TSS in next 3 vertical bars, TPS in next 3 vertical bars) across; work lps off hook.

Row 5: Skip first vertical bar, TSS in next vertical bar, TPS in next 4 vertical bars, (TSS in next 2 vertical bars, TPS in next 4 vertical bars) across; work lps off hook.

Row 6: Skip first vertical bar, TPS in next 5 vertical bars, (TSS in next vertical bar, TPS in next 5 vertical bars) across; work lps off hook.

Pattern Rows: Repeat rows 2–6 consecutively to desired size, ending with row 5.

Last Row: Skip first vertical bar, insert hook in next vertical bar, yo, pull lp through 2 lps on hook *(sl st completed),* sl st in each vertical bar across. Fasten off.❑❑

MATERIALS
❑ Desired color yarn
❑ Easy Tunisian hook

NOTE
Read Tunisian Information on pages 1–4 before beginning pattern.

STITCH PATTERN
Row 1: Ch a minimum of 4 or in multiples of 2, pull up lp in second ch from hook, pull up lp in each ch across, **do not turn;** work lps off hook.

Row 2: Skip first vertical bar, *insert hook in next 2 vertical bars at same time, yo, pull lp through, ch 1, pull up lp in top strand of next horizontal bar *(see illustration);* repeat from * across to last vertical bar, TSS in last vertical bar; work lps off hook.

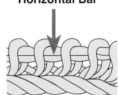

Horizontal Bar

Row 3: Ch 1, skip first vertical bar, (pull up lp in top strand of next horizontal bar, insert hook in next 2 vertical bars at same time, yo, pull lp through, ch 1) across to last vertical bar, TSS in last vertical bar; work lps off hook.

Pattern Rows: Repeat rows 2 and 3 alternately to desired size.

Last Row: Skip first vertical bar, insert hook in next vertical bar, yo, pull lp through 2 lps on hook *(sl st completed),* sl st in each vertical bar across. Fasten off.❑❑

MATERIALS
❑ Desired color yarn
❑ Easy Tunisian hook

NOTE
Read Tunisian Information on pages 1–4 before beginning pattern.

STITCH PATTERN
Row 1: Ch in multiples of 3, pull up lp in second ch from hook, pull up lp in each ch across, **do not turn;** work lps off hook.

Row 2: Skip first vertical bar, TSS

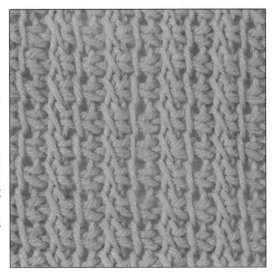

in next vertical bar, (skip next vertical bar, TSS in next vertical bar, TSS in skipped vertical bar, TSS in next vertical bar) across to last vertical bar, TSS in last vertical bar; work lps off hook.

Pattern Rows: Repeat row 2 to desired size.

Last Row: Skip first vertical bar, insert hook in next vertical bar, yo, pull lp through 2 lps on hook *(sl st completed),* sl st in each vertical bar across. Fasten off.❑❑

MATERIALS
❑ Desired color yarn
❑ Easy Tunisian hook

SPECIAL STITCH
For **treble crochet lp (tr lp),** yo 2 times, insert hook around post of specified st, yo, pull lp through, (yo, pull through 2 lps on hook) 2 times. Skip next vertical bar on last row behind tr lp.

NOTE
Read Tunisian Information on pages 1–4 before beginning pattern.

STITCH PATTERN
Row 1: Ch a minimum of 15 or in multiples of 4 plus 3, pull up lp in second ch from hook, pull up lp in each ch across, **do not turn;** work lps off hook.
Row 2: Work in TSS.

Row 3: Skip first vertical bar, TSS in next 2 vertical bars, ***tr lp** (see Special Stitch) around vertical bar on row before last directly below last TSS and next 2 vertical bars at same time (total of 3), TSS in next 3 vertical bars on last row; repeat from * across; work lps off hook.
Row 4: Work in TSS.
Row 5: Skip first vertical bar, TSS in next 4 vertical bars, (*tr lp around vertical bar on row before last directly below last TSS and next 2 vertical bars at same time (total of 3)*, TSS in next 3 vertical bars on last row); repeat between ( ) across to last 6 vertical bars; repeat between **, TSS in last 5 vertical bars; work lps off hook.
Pattern Rows: Repeat rows 2–5 consecutively to desired size, ending with row 3.
Last Row: Skip first vertical bar, insert hook in next vertical bar, yo, pull lp through 2 lps on hook (sl st completed), sl st in each vertical bar across. Fasten off.❑❑

MATERIALS
❑ Desired color yarn
❑ Easy Tunisian hook

NOTE
Read Tunisian Information on pages 1–4 before beginning pattern.

STITCH PATTERN
Row 1: Ch in multiples of 3 plus 2, pull up lp in second ch from hook, pull up lp in each ch across, **do not turn;** work lps off hook.
Row 2: Skip first vertical bar, *insert hook in next 3 vertical bars at same time, yo, pull lp through, TSS in center vertical bar of 3-bar group

just formed, TSS in first bar of same 3-bar group; repeat from * across to last vertical bar, TSS in last vertical bar; work lps off hook.
Pattern Rows: Repeat row 2 to desired size.
Last Row: Skip first vertical bar, *insert hook in next 3 vertical bars at same time, yo, pull through 2 lps on hook (sl st completed), sl st in center vertical bar of 3-bar group just formed, sl st in first bar of same 3-bar group; repeat from * across to last vertical bar, sl st in last vertical bar. Fasten off.❑❑

MATERIALS
❑ Desired color yarn
❑ Easy Tunisian hook

SPECIAL STITCH
For **double crochet lp (dc lp)**, yo, insert hook through work from front to back between strands of next vertical bar, yo, pull lp through, yo, pull through 2 lps on hook.

NOTE
Read Tunisian Information on pages 1–4 before beginning pattern.

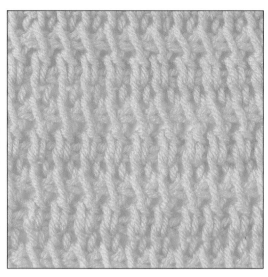

STITCH PATTERN
Row 1: Ch desired number, pull up lp in second ch from hook, pull up lp in each ch across, **do not turn;** work lps off hook.

Row 2: Ch 1, skip first vertical bar, **dc lp** *(see Special Stitch)* in each vertical bar across; work lps off hook.

Pattern Rows: Repeat row 2 to desired size.

Last Row: Skip first vertical bar, insert hook in next vertical bar, yo, pull through 2 lps on hook *(sl st completed)*, sl st in each vertical bar across. Fasten off.❑❑

MATERIALS
❑ Desired color yarn
❑ Easy Tunisian hook

NOTE
Read Tunisian Information on pages 1–4 before beginning pattern.

STITCH PATTERN
Row 1: Ch a minimum of 6 or in multiples of 3, pull up lp in second ch from hook, pull up lp in each ch across, **do not turn;** work lps off hook.

Row 2: Skip first vertical bar, TKS in next vertical bar, (skip next vertical bar, TSS in next vertical bar;

working in front of st just made, TSS in skipped vertical bar, TKS in next vertical bar) across to last vertical bar, TSS in last vertical bar; work lps off hook.

Pattern Rows: Repeat row 2 to desired size.

Last Row: Skip first vertical bar, insert hook from front to back between strands of next vertical bar, yo, pull through 2 lps on hook *(sl st completed)*, following TKS and TSS stitch pattern, sl st in each vertical bar across. Fasten off.❑❑

MATERIALS
- ❏ Desired color yarn
- ❏ Easy Tunisian hook

NOTE
Read Tunisian Information on pages 1–4 before beginning pattern.

STITCH PATTERN
Row 1: Ch a minimum of 8 or in multiples of 4, pull up lp in second ch from hook, pull up lp in each ch across, **do not turn;** work lps off hook.

Row 2: Skip first 2 vertical bars, TSS in next vertical bar; working in

front of st just made, TSS in second skipped vertical bar, (TKS in next 2 vertical bars, skip next vertical bar, TSS in next vertical bar; working in front of st just made, TSS in skipped vertical bar) across to last vertical bar, TSS in last vertical bar; work lps off hook.

Pattern Rows: Repeat row 2 to desired size.

Last Row: Skip first vertical bar, insert hook in next vertical bar, yo, pull through 2 lps on hook *(sl st completed)*, following TSS and TKS stitch pattern, sl st in each vertical bar across. Fasten off.❏❏

MATERIALS
- ❏ Desired color yarn
- ❏ Easy Tunisian hook

NOTE
Read Tunisian Information on pages 1–4 before beginning pattern.

STITCH PATTERN
Row 1: Ch a minimum of 11 or in multiples of 5 plus 1, pull up lp in second ch from hook, pull up lp in each ch across, **do not turn;** work lps off hook.

Row 2: Skip first 2 vertical bars, TSS in next vertical bar; working in front of st just made, TSS in second skipped vertical bar, skip next vertical bar.

TSS in next vertical bar; working in front of st just made, TSS in skipped vertical bar, *TPS in next vertical bar, (skip next vertical bar, TSS in next vertical bar; working in front of st just made, TSS in skipped vertical bar) 2 times; repeat from * across to last vertical bar, TSS in last vertical bar; work lps off hook.

Pattern Rows: Repeat row 2 to desired size.

Last Row: Skip first vertical bar, insert hook in next vertical bar, yo, pull through 2 lps on hook *(sl st completed)*, following TSS and TPS stitch pattern, sl st in each vertical bar across. Fasten off.❏❏

MATERIALS
❏ Desired color yarn
❏ Easy Tunisian hook

NOTE
Read Tunisian Information on pages 1–4 before beginning pattern.

STITCH PATTERN
Row 1: Ch a minimum of 5 or in multiples of 2 plus 1, pull up lp in second ch from hook, pull up lp in each ch across, **do not turn;** work lps off hook.
Row 2: Skip first vertical bar, (TPS in next vertical bar, TSS in next vertical bar) across; work lps off hook.

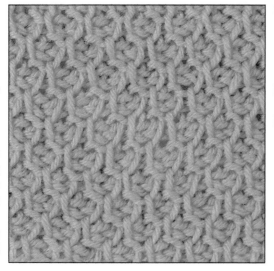

Row 3: Skip first vertical bar, (TSS in next vertical bar, TPS in next vertical bar) across to last 2 vertical bars, TSS in last 2 vertical bars; work lps off hook.
Pattern Rows: Repeat rows 2 and 3 alternately to desired size.
Last Row: Skip first vertical bar, *bring yarn to front of work; working behind yarn, insert hook under next vertical bar, yo, pull through 2 lps on hook *(sl st completed);* working in front of yarn, insert hook in next vertical bar, yo, pull through 2 lps on hook; repeat from * across. Fasten off.❏❏

MATERIALS
❏ Desired color yarn
❏ Easy Tunisian hook

NOTE
Read Tunisian Information on pages 1–4 before beginning pattern.

STITCH PATTERN
Row 1: Ch a minimum of 6 or in multiples of 2, pull up lp in second ch from hook, pull up lp in each ch across, **do not turn;** work lps off hook.
Rows 2 & 3: Skip first 2 vertical bars, TSS in next vertical bar; working in front of st just made, TSS in second skipped vertical bar, (skip next vertical bar, TSS in next vertical bar;

working in front of st just made, TSS in skipped vertical bar) across to last vertical bar, TSS in last vertical bar; work lps off hook.
Rows 4 & 5: Work in TKS.
Pattern Rows: Repeat rows 2–5 consecutively to desired size, ending with row 2.
Last Row: Skip first 2 vertical bars, insert hook in next vertical bar, yo, pull through 2 lps on hook *(sl st completed);* working in front of st just made, sl st in second skipped vertical bar, (skip next vertical bar, sl st in next vertical bar; working in front of st just made, sl st in skipped vertical bar) across to last vertical bar, sl st in last vertical bar. Fasten off.❏❏

MATERIALS
❑ Desired color yarn
❑ Easy Tunisian hook

NOTE
Read Tunisian Information on pages 1–4 before beginning pattern.

STITCH PATTERN
Row 1: Ch in multiples of 8 plus 4, pull up lp in second ch from hook, pull up lp in each ch across, **do not turn;** work lps off hook.

Rows 2–4: Skip first vertical bar, TPS in next 3 vertical bars, (TKS in next 4 vertical bars, TPS in next

4 vertical bars) across; work lps off hook.

Rows 5–7: Skip first vertical bar, TKS in next 3 vertical bars, (TPS in next 4 vertical bars, TKS in next 4 vertical bars) across; work lps off hook.

Pattern Rows: Repeat rows 2–7 consecutively to desired size, ending with row 4.

Last Row: Skip first vertical bar, insert hook in next vertical bar, yo, pull through 2 lps on hook *(sl st completed),* sl st in each vertical bar across. Fasten off.❑❑

MATERIALS
❑ Desired color yarn
❑ Easy Tunisian hook

NOTE
Read Tunisian Information on pages 1–4 before beginning pattern.

STITCH PATTERN
Row 1: Ch in multiples of 6 plus 3, pull up lp in second ch from hook, pull up lp in each ch across, **do not turn;** to **work lps off hook,** yo, pull through one lp on hook, (yo, pull through 2 lps on hook) 2 times, * ch 1, yo, pull through 4 lps on hook *(ch sp and shell made),* ch 1, (yo, pull through 2 lps on hook) 3 times; repeat from * across.

Row 2: Skip first vertical bar, TSS in next 2 vertical bars, (TSS in

next ch sp, TSS in horizontal bar at top of next shell, TSS in next ch sp, TSS in next 3 vertical bars) across; to **work lps off hook,** yo, pull through one lp on hook, (yo, pull through 2 lps on hook) 2 times, *ch 1, yo, pull through 4 lps on hook, ch 1, (yo, pull through 2 lps on hook) 3 times; repeat from * across.

Pattern Rows: Repeat row 2 to desired size.

Last Row: Skip first vertical bar, insert hook in next vertical bar, yo, pull through 2 lps on hook *(sl st completed),* sl st in each vertical bar, in each ch sp and in horizontal bar at top of each shell across. Fasten off.❑❑

MATERIALS
- ❑ Desired color yarn
- ❑ Easy Tunisian hook

NOTE
Read Tunisian Information on pages 1–4 before beginning pattern.

STITCH PATTERN
Row 1: Ch a minimum of 6 or in multiples of 2, pull up lp in second ch from hook, pull up lp in each ch across, **do not turn;** work lps off hook.

Row 2: Skip first 2 vertical bars, TSS in next vertical bar; working in front of st just made, TSS in second skipped vertical bar, (skip next vertical bar, TSS in next verti-cal bar; working in front of st just made, TSS in skipped vertical bar) across to last vertical bar, TSS in last vertical bar; work lps off hook.

Pattern Rows: Repeat row 2 to desired size.

Last Row: Skip first 2 vertical bars, insert hook in next vertical bar, yo, pull through 2 lps on hook (*sl st completed*); working in front of st just made, sl st in second skipped vertical bar, (skip next vertical bar, sl st in next vertical bar; working in front of st just made, sl st in skipped vertical bar) across to last vertical bar, sl st in last vertical bar. Fasten off.❑❑

MATERIALS
- ❑ Desired color yarn
- ❑ Easy Tunisian hook

SPECIAL STITCH
For **double crochet lp (dc lp),** yo, insert hook through work from front to back between strands of next vertical bar, yo, pull lp through, yo, pull through 2 lps on hook.

NOTE
Read Tunisian Information on pages 1–4 before beginning pattern.

STITCH PATTERN
Row 1: Ch a minimum of 5 or in multiples of 2 plus 1, pull up lp in second ch from hook, pull up lp

in each ch across, **do not turn;** work lps off hook.

Row 2: Skip first vertical bar, **dc lp** (*see Special Stitch*), TPS in next vertical bar, (dc lp, TPS in next vertical bar) across; work lps off hook.

Row 3: Skip first vertical bar, TPS in next vertical bar, (dc lp, TPS in next vertical bar) across to last vertical bar, TSS in last vertical bar; work lps off hook.

Pattern Rows: Repeat rows 2 and 3 alternately to desired size, end-ing with row 2.

Last Row: Skip first vertical bar, insert hook in next verti-cal bar, yo, pull through 2 lps on hook (*sl st completed*), sl st in each vertical bar across. Fasten off.❑❑

MATERIALS
❏ Desired color yarn
❏ Easy Tunisian hook

NOTE
Read Tunisian Information on pages 1–4 before beginning pattern.

STITCH PATTERN
Row 1: Ch in multiples of 3 plus 2, pull up lp in second ch from hook, pull up lp in each ch across, **do not turn;** work lps off hook.

Row 2: Skip first vertical bar, (yo, TSS in next 3 vertical bars, pull last yo over last 3 lps and off hook) across to last vertical bar, TSS in last vertical bar; work lps off hook.

Pattern Rows: Repeat row 2 to desired size.

Last Row: Skip first vertical bar, insert hook in next vertical bar, yo, pull through 2 lps on hook (*sl st completed*), sl st in each vertical bar across. Fasten off.❏❏

MATERIALS
❏ Desired color yarn
❏ Easy Tunisian hook

NOTE
Read Tunisian Information on pages 1–4 before beginning pattern.

STITCH PATTERN
Row 1: Ch a minimum of 12 or in multiples of 8 plus 4, pull up lp in second ch from hook, pull up lp in each ch

across, **do not turn;** work lps off hook.

Row 2: Skip first vertical bar, TSS in next 3 vertical bars, (TPS in next 4 vertical bars, TSS in next 4 vertical bars) across; work lps off hook.

Pattern Rows: Repeat row 2 to desired size.

Last Row: Skip first vertical bar, insert hook in next vertical bar, yo, pull through 2 lps on hook (*sl st completed*), sl st in each vertical bar across. Fasten off.❏❏

MATERIALS
- ❏ Desired color yarn
- ❏ Easy Tunisian hook

SPECIAL STITCH
For **chain loop stitch (ch lp st),** pull up lp in next vertical bar, ch 7; working behind ch-7 just made, pull up lp in top strand of horizontal bar at base of ch-7, yo, pull through 2 lps on hook.

NOTE
Read Tunisian Information on pages 1–4 before beginning pattern.

STITCH PATTERN
Row 1: Ch a minimum of 11 or in multiples of 4 plus 3, pull up lp in second ch from hook, pull

up lp in each ch across, **do not turn;** work lps off hook.

Row 2: Skip first vertical bar, TSS in next 2 vertical bars, **ch lp st** (see Special Stitch) in next vertical bar, TSS in next 3 vertical bars, (ch lp st in next vertical bar, TSS in next 3 vertical bars) across; work lps off hook.

Row 3: Work in TSS.

Row 4: Skip first vertical bar, TSS in next 2 vertical bars, (pull up lp in next ch lp, skip next vertical bar behind ch lp, TSS in next 3 vertical bars) across; work lps off hook.

Row 5: Work in TSS.

Pattern Rows: Repeat rows 2–5 consecutively to desired size, ending with row 4.

Last Row: Skip first vertical bar, insert hook in next vertical bar, yo, pull through 2 lps on hook (sl st completed), sl st in each vertical bar across. Fasten off.❏❏

MATERIALS
- ❏ Desired color yarn
- ❏ Easy Tunisian hook

NOTE
Read Tunisian Information on pages 1–4 before beginning pattern.

STITCH PATTERN
Row 1: Ch a minimum of 6 or in multiples of 2, pull up lp in second ch from hook, pull up lp in each ch across, **do not turn;** work lps off hook.

Row 2: Skip first vertical bar, TPS across to last vertical bar, TSS in last vertical bar; work lps off hook.

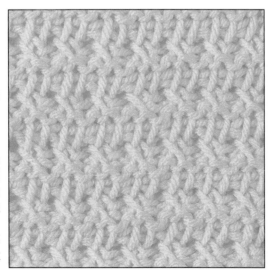

Row 3: Skip first 2 vertical bars, TSS in next vertical bar; working in front of st just made, TSS in second skipped vertical bar, (skip next vertical bar, TSS in next vertical bar; working in front of st just made, TSS in skipped vertical bar) across to last vertical bar, TSS in last vertical bar; work lps off hook.

Pattern Rows: Repeat rows 2 and 3 alternately to desired size, ending with row 2.

Last Row: Skip first vertical bar, insert hook in next vertical bar, yo, pull through 2 lps on hook (sl st completed), sl st in each vertical bar across. Fasten off.❏❏

MATERIALS
❑ Desired color yarn
❑ Easy Tunisian hook

NOTES
Read Tunisian Information on pages 1–4 before beginning pattern.

This stitch pattern causes the fabric to bias or angle very badly; therefore, it is necessary to decrease at the beginning and increase at the end of every other row.

STITCH PATTERN
Row 1: Ch in multiples of 2, yo, pull up lp in second ch from hook, yo, pull up lp in each ch across, **do not turn** (number of lps left on hook will be number of starting chs multiplied by 2 minus 1); to **work lps off hook,** yo, pull through first 2 lps on hook, (yo, pull through 3 lps on hook) across to last 2 lps on hook, yo, pull through last 2 lps on hook.

Row 2: Skip first vertical bar, (yo, insert hook in next 2 vertical bars at same time, yo, pull lp through) across; to **work lps off hook,** yo, pull through first 2 lps on hook, (yo, pull through 3 lps on hook) across to last 2 lps on hook, yo, pull through last 2 lps on hook.

Row 3: Skip first 3 vertical bars (decrease completed), (yo, insert hook in next 2 vertical bars at same time, yo, pull lp through) across to last 2 vertical bars, yo, insert hook in top strand of next horizontal bar (see illustration), yo, pull lp through (increase completed), yo, insert hook in last 2 vertical bars at same time, yo, pull lp through; to **work lps off hook,** yo, pull through first 2 lps on hook, (yo, pull through 3 lps on hook) across to last 2 lps on hook, yo, pull through last 2 lps on hook.

Horizontal Bar

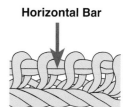

Pattern Rows: Repeat rows 2 and 3 alternately to desired size.

Last Row: Skip first vertical bar, insert hook in next 2 vertical bars at same time, yo, pull through 2 lps on hook (sl st completed), (sl st in next 2 vertical bars at same time) across. Fasten off.❑❑

MATERIALS
❑ Desired color yarn
❑ Easy Tunisian hook

NOTE
Read Tunisian Information on pages 1–4 before beginning pattern.

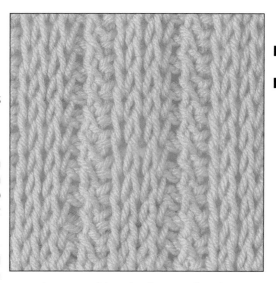

STITCH PATTERN
Row 1: Ch a minimum of 9 or in multiples of 5 plus 4, pull up lp in second ch from hook, pull up lp in each ch across, **do not turn;** work lps off hook.

Row 2: Skip first 2 vertical bars, TSS in next vertical bar; working in front of st just made, TSS in second skipped vertical bar, (TKS in next 3 vertical bars, skip next vertical bar, TSS in next vertical bar; working in front of st just made, TSS in skipped vertical bar) across to last vertical bar, TSS in last vertical bar; work lps off hook.

Pattern Rows: Repeat row 2 to desired size.

Last Row: Skip first 2 vertical bars, insert hook in next vertical bar, yo, pull through 2 lps on hook (sl st completed); working in front of st just made, sl st in second skipped vertical bar, *(insert hook through work from front to back between strands of next vertical bar, yo, pull through 2 lps on hook) 3 times, skip next vertical bar, sl st in next vertical bar; working in front of st just made, sl st in skipped vertical bar; repeat from * across to last vertical bar, sl st in last vertical bar. Fasten off.❑❑

MATERIALS
❑ Desired color yarn
❑ Easy Tunisian hook

NOTE
Read Tunisian Information on pages 1–4 before beginning pattern.

STITCH PATTERN
Row 1: Ch a minimum of 6 or in multiples of 2, pull up lp in second ch from hook, pull up lp in each ch across, **do not turn;** work lps off hook.

Row 2: Skip first 2 vertical bars, TSS in next vertical bar, ch 1; working in front of st just made, TSS in second skipped vertical bar, ch 1, (skip next

vertical bar, TSS in next vertical bar, ch 1; working in front of st just made, TSS in skipped vertical bar, ch 1) across to last vertical bar, TSS in last vertical bar; work lps off hook.

Pattern Rows: Repeat row 2 to desired size.

Last Row: Skip first 2 vertical bars, insert hook in next vertical bar, yo, pull through 2 lps on hook *(sl st completed);* working in front of st just made, sl st in second skipped vertical bar, (skip next vertical bar, sl st in next vertical bar; working in front of st just made, sl st in skipped vertical bar) across to last vertical bar, sl st in last vertical bar. Fasten off.❑❑

MATERIALS
❑ Desired color yarn
❑ Easy Tunisian hook

NOTE
Read Tunisian Information on pages 1–4 before beginning pattern.

STITCH PATTERN
Row 1: Ch a minimum of 8 or in multiples of 4, pull up lp in second ch from hook, pull up lp in each ch across, **do not turn;** work lps off hook.

Row 2: Skip first 2 vertical bars, TSS in next vertical bar; working in front of st just made, TSS in second skipped vertical bar, (TPS in next 2 vertical bars, skip next vertical bar, TSS in next vertical

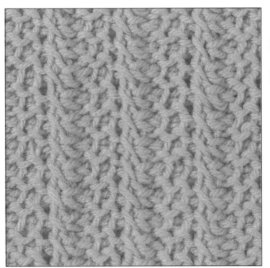

bar; working in front of st just made, TSS in skipped vertical bar) across to last vertical bar,

TSS in last vertical bar; work lps off hook.

Pattern Rows: Repeat row 2 to desired size.

Last Row: Skip first 2 vertical bars, insert hook in next vertical bar, yo, pull through 2 lps on hook *(sl st completed);* working in front of st just made, sl st in second skipped vertical bar, *(bring yarn to front of work; working behind yarn, insert hook in next vertical bar, yo, pull through 2 lps on hook) 2 times, skip next vertical bar, sl st in next vertical bar; working in front of st just made, sl st in skipped vertical bar; repeat from * across to last vertical bar, sl st in last vertical bar. Fasten off.❑❑

MATERIALS
❑ Desired color yarn
❑ Easy Tunisian hook

SPECIAL STITCH
For **extended double crochet loop (ext dc lp),** yo, insert hook around both strands at base of specified vertical bar, yo, pull lp through, yo, pull through 2 lps on hook, yo, pull through one lp on hook.

NOTE
Read Tunisian Information on pages 1–4 before beginning pattern.

STITCH PATTERN
Row 1: Ch a minimum of 8 or in multiples of 4, pull up lp in second ch from hook, pull up lp in each ch across, **do not turn;** work lps off hook.
Row 2: Work in TSS.
Row 3: Skip first vertical bar, **ext**

dc lp (see Special Stitch) around next 2 vertical bars on row before last, (TSS in next 2 vertical bars on last row, ext dc lp around next 2 vertical bars on row before last) across to last vertical bar, TSS in last vertical bar; work lps off hook.
Row 4: Work in TSS.

Row 5: Skip first vertical bar, TSS in next 2 vertical bars, (ext dc lp around next 2 vertical bars on row before last, TSS in next 2 vertical bars on last row) across to last vertical bar, TSS in last vertical bar; work lps off hook.
Pattern Rows: Repeat rows 2–5 consecutively to desired size, ending with row 4.
Last Row: Skip first vertical bar, insert hook in next vertical bar, yo, pull through 2 lps on hook (sl st completed), *yo, insert hook around both strands at base of vertical bar on row before last, yo, pull lp through, (yo, pull through 2 lps on hook) 2 times, skip next st on last row behind dc just made*; repeat between **, [sl st in next 2 vertical bars; repeat between ** 2 more times]; repeat between [ ] across to last vertical bar, sl st in last vertical bar. Fasten off.❑❑

MATERIALS
❑ Desired color yarn
❑ Easy Tunisian hook

NOTE
Read Tunisian Information on pages 1–4 before beginning pattern.

STITCH PATTERN
Row 1: Ch a minimum of 8 or in multiples of 4, pull up lp in second ch from hook, pull up lp in each ch across, **do not turn;** work lps off hook.
Row 2: Skip first 2 vertical bars, TSS in next vertical bar; working in front of st just made, TSS in second skipped vertical bar, (TSS in next 2 vertical bars, skip next

vertical bar, TSS in next vertical bar; working in front of st just

made, TSS in skipped vertical bar) across to last vertical bar, TSS in last vertical bar; work lps off hook.
Pattern Rows: Repeat row 2 to desired size.
Last Row: Skip first 2 vertical bars, insert hook in next vertical bar, yo, pull through 2 lps on hook (sl st completed); working in front of st just made, sl st in second skipped vertical bar, (sl st in next 2 vertical bars, skip next vertical bar, sl st in next vertical bar; working in front of st just made, sl st in skipped vertical bar) across to last vertical bar, sl st in last vertical bar. Fasten off.❑❑

MATERIALS
- ❑ Two desired colors of yarn (color A and color B)
- ❑ Easy Tunisian hook

SPECIAL STITCH
For **double crochet lp (dc lp),** yo, insert hook under specified vertical bar on row before last, yo, pull lp through, yo, pull through 2 lps on hook. Skip next st on last row behind dc lp.

NOTES
Read Tunisian Information on pages 1–4 before beginning pattern.

When changing colors *(see illustration),* carry dropped color loosely across ends of rows until needed.

STITCH PATTERN
Row 1: With A, ch a minimum of 5 or in multiples of 2 plus 1, pull

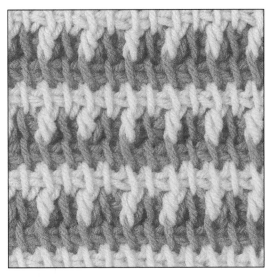

up lp in second ch from hook, pull up lp in each ch across, **do not turn;** work lps off hook.

Row 2: Work in TSS changing to B in last st made.

Row 3: Skip first vertical bar, **dc lp** *(see Special Stitch)* in next vertical bar on row before last, TSS in next vertical bar on last row, (dc lp in next vertical bar on row before last, TSS in next vertical bar on last row) across; work lps off hook changing to A in last st made.

Rows 4 & 5: Work in TSS. At end of last row, change to B in last st made.

Pattern Rows: Repeat rows 3–5 consecutively to desired size.

Last Row: Skip first vertical bar, insert hook in next vertical bar, yo, pull through 2 lps on hook *(sl st completed);* sl st in each vertical bar across. Fasten off.❑❑

MATERIALS
- ❑ Desired color yarn
- ❑ Easy Tunisian hook

NOTE
Read Tunisian Information on pages 1–4 before beginning pattern.

STITCH PATTERN
Row 1: Ch a minimum of 11 or in multiples of 5 plus 1, pull up lp in second ch from hook, pull up lp in each ch across, **do not turn;** work lps off hook.

Row 2: Skip first 2 vertical bars, TSS in next vertical bar; working in front of st just made, TSS in second skipped vertical bar, skip next vertical bar, TSS in next vertical bar; working in front of st just made, TSS in skipped verti-

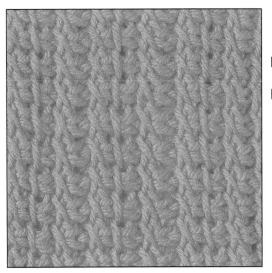

cal bar, TSS in next vertical bar, *(skip next vertical bar, TSS in next vertical bar; working in front of st just made, TSS in skipped vertical

bar) 2 times, TSS in next vertical bar; repeat from * across; work lps off hook.

Pattern Rows: Repeat row 2 to desired size.

Last Row: Skip first 2 vertical bars, insert hook in next vertical bar, yo, pull through 2 lps on hook *(sl st completed);* working in front of st just made, sl st in second skipped vertical bar, skip next vertical bar, sl st in next vertical bar; working in front of st just made, sl st in skipped vertical bar, sl st in next vertical bar, *(skip next vertical bar, sl st in next vertical bar; working in front of st just made, sl st in skipped vertical bar) 2 times, sl st in next vertical bar; repeat from * across. Fasten off.❑❑

MATERIALS
❏ Desired color yarn
❏ Easy Tunisian hook

SPECIAL STITCH
For **extended single crochet loop (esc lp),** yo, insert hook from front to back between strands of next vertical bar or in specified sp, yo, pull lp through, yo, pull through one lp on hook, yo, pull through 2 lps on hook.

NOTE
Read Tunisian Information on pages 1–4 before beginning pattern.

STITCH PATTERN
Row 1: Ch a minimum of 9 or in multiples of 6 plus 3, pull up lp in second ch from hook, pull up lp in each ch across, **do not turn;** work lps off hook.

Row 2: Ch 1, skip first vertical bar, (pull up lp in next vertical bar, ch 1) 2 times, *skip next vertical bar, 2 esc lps *(see Special Stitch)* in next vertical bar, skip next vertical bar, (pull up lp in next vertical bar, ch 1) 3 times; repeat from * across; to **work lps off hook,** yo, pull through one lp on hook, (yo, pull through 2 lps on hook) 2 times, [ch 1, (yo, pull through 2 lps on hook) 2 times, ch 1, (yo, pull through 2 lps on hook) 3 times]; repeat between [ ] across.

Row 3: Ch 1, skip first vertical bar, (pull up lp in next vertical bar, ch 1) 2 times, *2 esc lps in sp between next 2 esc lps, skip next vertical bar, (pull up lp in next vertical bar, ch 1) 3 times; repeat from * across; to **work lps off hook,** yo, pull through one lp on hook, (yo, pull through 2 lps on hook) 2 times, [ch 1, (yo, pull through 2 lps on hook) 2 times, ch 1, (yo, pull through 2 lps on hook) 3 times]; repeat between [ ] across.

Pattern Rows: Repeat row 3 to desired size.

Last Row: Skip first vertical bar, insert hook in next vertical bar, yo, pull through 2 lps on hook *(sl st completed),* sl st in next 2 vertical bars, (sl st in next ch, sl st in sp between next 2 esc lps, skip next esc lp, sl st in next ch, sl st in next 3 vertical bars) across. Fasten off.❏❏

MATERIALS
❏ Desired color yarn
❏ Easy Tunisian hook

NOTE
Read Tunisian Information on pages 1–4 before beginning pattern.

STITCH PATTERN
Row 1: Ch a minimum of 6 or in multiples of 3, pull up lp in second ch from hook, pull up lp in each ch across, **do not turn;** work lps off hook.

Row 2: Skip first vertical bar, TPS in next vertical bar, (skip next vertical bar, TSS in next vertical bar; working in front of st just made, TSS in skipped vertical bar, TPS in next vertical bar) across to last vertical bar, TSS in last vertical bar; work lps off hook.

Pattern Rows: Repeat row 2 to desired size.

Last Row: Skip first vertical bar, bring yarn to front of work; working behind yarn, insert hook in next vertical bar, yo, pull through 2 lps on hook *(p sl st completed),* *skip next vertical bar, insert hook in next vertical bar, yo, pull through 2 lps on hook *(sl st completed);* working in front of st just made, sl st in skipped vertical bar, p sl st in next vertical bar; repeat from * across to last vertical bar, sl st in last vertical bar. Fasten off.❏❏

MATERIALS
❑ Desired color yarn
❑ Easy Tunisian hook

NOTE
Read Tunisian Information on pages 1–4 before beginning pattern.

STITCH PATTERN
Row 1: Ch a minimum of 6 or in multiples of 2, pull up lp in second ch from hook, pull up lp in each ch across, **do not turn;** work lps off hook.

Row 2: Skip first 2 vertical bars, TSS in next vertical bar; working in front of st just made, TSS

in second skipped vertical bar, (skip next vertical bar, TSS in next vertical bar; working in front of st just made, TSS in skipped vertical bar) across to last vertical bar, TSS in last vertical bar; work lps off hook.

Row 3: Work in TSS.

Pattern Rows: Repeat rows 2 and 3 alternately to desired size, ending with row 2.

Last Row: Skip first vertical bar, insert hook under next vertical bar, yo, pull through 2 lps on hook (*sl st completed*), sl st in each vertical bar across. Fasten off.❑❑

MATERIALS
❑ Desired color yarn
❑ Easy Tunisian hook

NOTE
Read Tunisian Information on pages 1–4 before beginning pattern.

STITCH PATTERN
Row 1: Ch a minimum of 6 or in multiples of 3, pull up lp in second ch from hook, pull up lp in each ch across, **do not turn;** work lps off hook.

Row 2: Skip first vertical bar, (TKS in next vertical bar, TPS in next 2 vertical bars) across to last 2

vertical bars, TKS in last 2 vertical bars; work lps off hook.

Pattern Rows: Repeat row 2 to desired size.

Last Row: Skip first vertical bar, insert hook through work from front to back between strands of next vertical bar, yo, pull through 2 lps on hook (*k sl st completed*), bring yarn to front of work; working behind yarn, insert hook in next vertical bar, yo, pull through 2 lps on hook (*p sl st completed*), p sl st in next vertical bar, (k sl st in next vertical bar, p sl st in next 2 vertical bars) across to last 2 vertical bars, k sl st in last 2 vertical bars. Fasten off.❑❑

MATERIALS
❑ Desired color yarn
❑ Easy Tunisian hook

NOTE
Read Tunisian Information on pages 1–4 before beginning pattern.

STITCH PATTERN
Row 1: Ch a minimum of 11 or in multiples of 5 plus 1, pull up lp in second ch from hook, pull up lp in each ch across, **do not turn;** work lps off hook.

Row 2: Skip first 2 vertical bars, TSS in next vertical bar; working in front of st just made, TSS in second skipped vertical bar, skip next vertical bar, TSS in next vertical bar; working in front of st just made, TSS in skipped vertical bar, *TKS in next verti-

cal bar, (skip next vertical bar, TSS in next vertical bar; working in front of st just made, TSS in skipped vertical bar) 2 times; repeat from * across to last verti-

cal bar, TSS in last vertical bar; work lps off hook.

Pattern Rows: Repeat row 2 to desired size.

Last Row: Skip first 2 vertical bars, insert hook in next vertical bar, yo, pull through 2 lps on hook *(sl st completed);* working in front of st just made, sl st in second skipped vertical bar, skip next vertical bar, sl st in next vertical bar; working in front of st just made, sl st in skipped vertical bar, *insert hook through work from front to back between strands of next vertical bar, yo, pull through 2 lps on hook *(k sl st completed),* (skip next vertical bar, sl st in next vertical bar; working in front of st just made, sl st in skipped vertical bar) 2 times; repeat from * across to last vertical bar, sl st in last vertical bar. Fasten off.❑❑

MATERIALS
❑ Two desired colors of yarn *(color A and color B)*
❑ Easy Tunisian hook

NOTES
Read Tunisian Information on pages 1–4 before beginning pattern.

When changing colors *(see illustration),* carry dropped color loosely across ends of rows until needed.

STITCH PATTERN
Row 1: With A, ch a minimum of 5 or in multiples of 2 plus 1, pull up lp in second ch from hook, pull up lp in each ch across, **do not turn;** work lps off hook changing

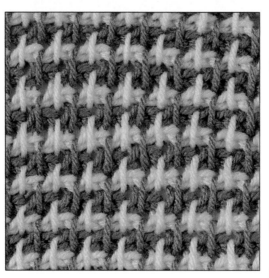

to B in last st made.

Row 2: Skip first vertical bar, slip next vertical bar on hook *(do not pull lp through, just place bar on hook),* (pull up lp in horizontal bar slightly above and behind next vertical bar, slip next vertical bar on hook) across to last vertical

bar, TSS in last vertical bar; work lps off hook changing to A in last st made.

Row 3: Skip first vertical bar, pull up lp in horizontal bar slightly above and behind next vertical bar, (slip next vertical bar on hook, pull up lp in horizontal bar slightly above and behind next vertical bar) across to last vertical bar, TSS in last vertical bar; work lps off hook, changing to B in last st made.

Pattern Rows: Repeat rows 2 and 3 alternately to desired size, ending with row 2.

Last Row: Skip first vertical bar, insert hook in horizontal bar slightly above and behind next vertical bar, yo, pull through 2 lps on hook *(sl st completed),* (sl st in next vertical bar, sl st in horizontal bar slightly above and behind next vertical bar) across to last vertical bar, sl st in last vertical bar. Fasten off.❑❑

MATERIALS
- ❏ Two desired colors of yarn (color A and color B)
- ❏ Easy Tunisian hook

NOTES
Read Tunisian Information on pages 1–4 before beginning pattern.

When changing colors *(see illustration)*, carry dropped color loosely across ends of rows until needed.

STITCH PATTERN
Row 1: With a minimum of 5 or in multiples of 2 plus 1, pull up lp in second ch from hook, pull up lp in each ch across, **do not turn;** work lps off hook changing to B in last st made.

Row 2: Skip first vertical bar, slip next vertical bar on hook *(do not*

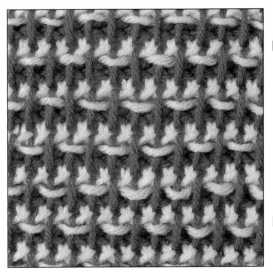

pull lp through, just place bar on hook), *bring yarn to **front** of work; working behind yarn, slip next vertical bar on hook, bring yarn to **back** of work; working in front of yarn, slip next vertical bar on hook; repeat from * across to last vertical bar, TSS in last vertical bar; work lps off hook changing to A in last st made.

Row 3: Skip first vertical bar, pull up lp in horizontal bar slightly above and behind each vertical bar across; work lps off hook changing to B in last st made.

Row 4: Skip first vertical bar, bring yarn to **front** of work; working behind yarn, slip next vertical bar on hook, *bring yarn to **back** of work; working in front of yarn, slip next vertical bar on hook, bring yarn to **front** of work; working behind yarn, slip next vertical bar on hook; repeat from * across to last vertical bar, TSS in last vertical bar; work lps off hook changing to A in last st made.

Row 5: Skip first vertical bar, pull up lp in horizontal bar slightly above and behind each vertical bar across; work lps off hook changing to B in last st made.

Pattern Rows: Repeat rows 2–5 consecutively to desired size, ending with row 2.

Last Row: Skip first vertical bar, insert hook in horizontal bar slightly above and behind next vertical bar, yo, pull through 2 lps on hook *(sl st completed),* sl st in horizontal bar slightly above and behind each vertical bar across to last vertical bar, sl st in last vertical bar. Fasten off.❏❏

MATERIALS
❑ Two desired colors of yarn (color A and color B)
❑ Easy Tunisian hook)

NOTES
Read Tunisian Information on pages 1–4 before beginning pattern.

When changing colors (see illustration), carry dropped color loosely across ends of rows until needed.

STITCH PATTERN
Row 1: With A, ch a minimum of 6 or in multiples of 2 (this will achieve an odd number of sts), pull up lp in third ch from hook, ch 1, (pull up lp in next ch, ch 1) across, **do not turn;** work lps off hook changing to B in last st made.

Row 2: Ch 1, skip first vertical bar,

slip next vertical bar on hook (do not pull lp through, just place bar on hook), *bring yarn to **front** of work; working behind yarn, slip next vertical bar on hook, bring yarn to **back** of work; working in front of yarn, slip next vertical bar on hook; repeat from * across to last vertical bar, pull up lp in last vertical bar, ch 1; work lps off hook.

Row 3: Ch 1, skip first vertical bar,

(pull up lp in next vertical bar, ch 1) across; work lps off hook changing to A in last st made.

Row 4: Ch 1, skip first vertical bar, bring yarn to **front** of work; working behind yarn, slip next vertical bar on hook, *bring yarn to **back** of work; working in front of yarn, slip next vertical bar on hook, bring yarn to **front** of work; working behind yarn, slip next vertical bar on hook; repeat from * across to last vertical bar, bring yarn to **back** of work; working in front of yarn, pull up lp in last vertical bar, ch 1; work lps off hook.

Row 5: Ch 1, skip first vertical bar, (pull up lp in next vertical bar, ch 1) across; work lps off hook changing to B in last st made.

Pattern Rows: Repeat rows 2–5 consecutively to desired size, ending with row 4.

Last Row: Ch 1, insert hook in first vertical bar, yo, pull lp through, yo, pull through 2 lps on hook (sc completed), sc in each vertical bar across. Fasten off.❑❑

MATERIALS
❑ Desired color yarn
❑ Easy Tunisian hook

NOTE
Read Tunisian Information on pages 1–4 before beginning pattern.

STITCH PATTERN
Row 1: Ch desired number or chs plus 1, pull up lp in third ch from hook, ch 1, (pull up lp in next ch, ch 1) across, **do not turn;** work lps off hook.

Row 2: Ch 1, skip first vertical bar and next horizontal bar, (insert hook in next vertical bar and in top strand of next horizontal bar at same time—see illustration, yo,

pull through 2 lps on hook, ch 1) across to last vertical bar, pull up

lp in last vertical bar, ch 1; work lps off hook.

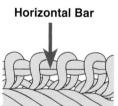

Horizontal Bar

Pattern Rows: Repeat row 2 to desired size.

Last Row: Ch 1, insert hook in first vertical bar, yo, pull through 2 lps on hook (sl st completed), sl st in each vertical bar across. Fasten off.❑❑

MATERIALS
❑ Two desired colors of yarn *(color A and color B)*
❑ Easy Tunisian hook

NOTE
Read Tunisian Information on pages 1–4 before beginning pattern.

STITCH PATTERN
Row 1: With A, ch desired number, pull up lp in second ch from hook, pull up lp in each ch across, **do not turn;** work lps off hook.

Row 2: Work in TSS.

Pattern Rows: Repeat row 2 to desired size.

Last Row: Skip first vertical bar,

insert hook in next vertical bar, pull through 2 lps on hook *(sl st*

completed), sl st in each vertical bar across. Fasten off.

For **embellishment,** use hook size necessary to keep sts flat and smooth and make sure they are neither too loose nor too tight.

Hold yarn at back of work and hook in front when working sl sts.

With yarn in back, insert hook from front to back through crocheted piece, pull slip knot through to front, insert hook in next st or row, yo, pull lp through fabric and lp on hook *(sl st completed),* continue to sl st design over crocheted piece as desired.

(It may help to graph or draw your design on paper before beginning.)❑❑

306 East Parr Road
Berne IN, 46711
© 2004 Annie's Attic

TOLL-FREE ORDER LINE or to request a free catalog (800) LV-ANNIE (800-582-6643)
Customer Service (800) AT-ANNIE (800-282-6643), **Fax** (800) 882-6643, **Pattern Services** (260) 589-4000, ext. 333
Visit www.AnniesAttic.com

ISBN: 1-931171-74-2   Printed in USA   4 5 6 7 8 9